CONTEMPORARY PIRACY AND MARITIME TERRORISM
The threat to international security

MARTIN N. MURPHY

ADELPHI PAPER 388

The International Institute for Strategic Studies

Arundel House | 13–15 Arundel Street | Temple Place | London | WC2R 3DX | UK

ADELPHI PAPER 388

First published July 2007 by **Routledge**
4 Park Square, Milton Park, Abingdon, Oxon, OX14 4RN

for **The International Institute for Strategic Studies**
Arundel House, 13–15 Arundel Street, Temple Place, London, WC2R 3DX, UK
www.iiss.org

Simultaneously published in the USA and Canada by **Routledge**
270 Madison Ave., New York, NY 10016

Routledge is an imprint of Taylor & Francis, an Informa Business

© 2007 The International Institute for Strategic Studies

DIRECTOR-GENERAL AND CHIEF EXECUTIVE John Chipman
EDITOR Tim Huxley
MANAGER FOR EDITORIAL SERVICES Ayse Abdullah
ASSISTANT EDITOR Katharine Fletcher
PRODUCTION John Buck
COVER IMAGE PA Photos

Printed and bound in Great Britain by Bell & Bain Ltd, Thornliebank, Glasgow

British Library Cataloguing in Publication Data
A catalogue record for this book is available from the British Library

Library of Congress Cataloging in Publication Data

ISBN 978-0-415-45234-2
ISSN 0567-932X

Contents

GLOSSARY

ASG	Abu Sayyaf Group
DIS	Defence Intelligence Staff (UK)
EEZ	Exclusive Economic Zone
FARC	Revolutionary Armed Forces of Colombia
FP-25	Popular Forces of April 25
GAM	Gerakan Aceh Merdeka
GRT	Gross Registered Tonnes
ICC	International Chamber of Commerce
ICU	Islamic Courts Union
IDF	Israel Defense Forces
IED	Improvised Explosive Device
IMB	International Maritime Bureau
IMO	International Maritime Organisation
IRA	Irish Republican Army
ISC	Information Sharing Centre
JIT	Just-In-Time delivery system
JWC	Joint War Committee
LNG	Liquefied Natural Gas
LPG	Liquefied Petroleum Gas
LTTE	Liberation Tigers of Tamil Eelam
MANPADS	Man-Portable Air Defence Systems
MARLO	US Maritime Liaison Office, Bahrain
MDA	Maritime Domain Awareness
MILF	Moro Islamic Liberation Front
MNLF	Moro National Liberation Front
NUMAST	National Union of Maritime, Aviation and Shipping Transport Officers

OECD	Organisation for Economic Cooperation and Development
ONI	Office of Naval Intelligence
PER	Perceived Enhanced Risk
PLO	Palestine Liberation Organisation
PRC	Piracy Reporting Centre
PSI	Proliferation Security Initiative
ReCAAP	Regional Cooperation Agreement on Combating Piracy and Armed Robbery Against Ships in Asia
RPG	Rocket-Propelled Grenade
SLN	Sri Lankan Navy
SUA	Convention for the Suppression of Unlawful Acts Against the Safety of Maritime Navigation
TSN	Thousand-Ship Navy
UNCLOS	United Nations Convention on the Law of the Sea

INTRODUCTION

As a largely unregulated space, the sea is potentially an environment that is especially vulnerable to terrorist attack, and since the 11 September attacks on New York and Washington, military and civilian analysts have been investigating the possibility of an event of a similar magnitude taking place at sea. A few major assaults on maritime targets in recent years have focused attention, particularly in the US, on what terrorists can achieve at sea, notably al-Qaeda's attacks on a US warship, the USS *Cole*, in Aden harbour in 2000 and the oil tanker MV *Limburg*, also off Yemen, in 2002; and the bombing of the *SuperFerry 14* passenger ferry in Manila by Philippine Islamist separatists in 2004, which killed 116 people.

In addition, there has been speculation that terrorists might undermine the world's seaborne trade in energy, raw materials and manufactured goods. In this context a connection with the perennial problem of piracy has been postulated. It has been suggested that in those parts of the world where piracy is prevalent pirates might deliberately help terrorists by teaching them the tricks of their trade, or unwittingly aid them by enabling preparations for terror attacks to look like incidents of ordinary piracy.

One report in particular crystallised these fears. In October 2003 a story in *The Economist*, amplified subsequently by an article in *Foreign Affairs*, reported that in March that year, terrorists had hijacked a chemical tanker off the coast of Sumatra using pirate techniques and then manoeuvred the vessel as if learning how to control it.[1] According to the report the 'pirates' or 'terrorists' had taken control of the *Dewi Madrim* for about an hour and during that time had altered course and speed but had left with little of value. The conclusion drawn was that they had been learning to control a ship in the same way that the 11 September hijackers had learnt to fly aircraft, possibly with a similar purpose in mind. This account originated with a London-based security consultancy, Aegis Defence Services, which suggested that 'something altogether more sinister' than a pirate attack had taken place and that terrorists could 'capture tug boats and tow … [a tanker] into a busy international port … and detonate the ship's contents'.[2] However, the ship's owner contradicted this and expressed the view that the attack was the work of pirates.[3] Extensive inquiries by the International Maritime Bureau (IMB), the branch of the International Chambers of Commerce that specialises in tackling international maritime crime and fraud, and other interested agencies could find no evidence to support the contention that terrorists had been involved.[4] What had taken place had been a standard pirate attack. The pirates had manoeuvred the vessel to stop it colliding with other ships or running aground while they stole what they could from it.[5] Aegis subsequently issued a second report, which warned that terrorists could adopt pirates' tactics or 'piggyback' on pirates' raids. It stated that 'the threat is not from traditional commercial pirates, but from a new breed of maritime terrorist, whose skills evolve from a conventional piracy base'.[6]

It is true that in the past couple of decades some terrorist organisations have collaborated and converged with groups of organised criminals such as drug traffickers, usually for financial reasons. Sometimes terrorist organisations have largely abandoned their political activities, effectively transforming themselves into criminal organisations. However, such relationships would seem not in fact to have come about between pirates and terrorists, although in some parts of the world, notably Southeast Asia, there are active terrorist groups that behave at times like pirates.

This paper will outline the main characteristics of piracy and maritime terrorism, and attempt to determine how much, individually or together, they present a threat to international security. It will not posit links where none exist. Violent criminal and political threats against maritime targets and the use that terrorists have made of the sea to advance their land campaigns will be the focus of the analysis. It is important to remember at this point that terrorism is a tactic, and that many of the groups that employ it are better viewed as insurgents than simply as 'terrorists'. For this reason, this paper uses the terms 'terrorist' and 'insurgent' interchangeably, although this usage should not be taken to be an implication that all insurgent groups make use of terror.

Figure 1 **Conditions that enable piracy and maritime terrorism**	
Piracy	**Maritime Terrorism**
Legal and jurisdictional weakness	Legal and jurisdictional weakness
Favourable geography	Geographical necessity
Conflict and disorder	
Under-funded law enforcement	Inadequate security
	Secure base areas
Cultural acceptability	Maritime tradition
	Charismatic and effective leadership
Permissive political environment	State support
Potential for reward	Potential for reward

There are a number of conditions that enable both piracy and maritime terrorism to flourish; in their absence, both would probably be unsustainable. Where circumstances favouring the two differ, the difference can be one of nuance (see Figure 1).

These conditions interact with one another, and although one or some will predominate at a given time or in a given place, all are usually present in some degree wherever piracy or maritime terrorism are found. How they work to enable piracy and terrorism to function will be examined in detail later. It is important to remember at this point that shared circumstances do not necessitate shared activity or cooperation between groups who are usually motivated by very different considerations.

Political context is the over-arching common factor. While this might be clear in relation to insurgency and terrorism, especially given the fact that weak states are less capable than others of resisting insurgent or terrorist infiltration, it may perhaps be less evident in the case of piracy. Yet the fortunes of piracy have always been intertwined with the power, fortunes and policies of states. Economic historian J.L. Anderson observed that 'throughout history, many officials at all levels of authority have found it expedient and usually profitable to ignore or even covertly to sponsor acts of piracy'.[7] What was true historically in England, France and America has been recognisable in our own times in China, Indonesia and the Philippines. Piracy is an organised crime. Even at its lowest level it requires a group and some connections on land to function. As far as international security is concerned, the more organised piracy becomes, the more dangerous it is, because organised crime feeds the political corruption that can destabilise states.

If piracy and maritime terrorism overlap it is in exploiting, alongside other criminal activities, the unregulated character of the high seas. In the case of states that are unable or unwilling to control what occurs in their territorial waters, the unregulated space extends right up to the coast. The coming together of criminals and terrorists is a recognised phenomenon that can, paradoxically, be welcomed by law enforcement organisations. The lower level of operational security at which criminals like smugglers generally work exposes their terrorist partners or customers to scrutiny if it takes place in an environment that has effective law enforcement.[8] However, when the space is unregulated and law enforcement bodies are largely absent, as they are at sea, this scrutiny is lacking.

Consequently, it is the generalised problem of disorder at sea that encourages maritime criminality and gives insurgents and terrorists the opportunity to pursue their activities largely unmolested by law enforcement. This problem will be exacerbated by the increasing pressure on coastal waters from what can be termed 'migration to the sea', as increasing numbers seek to exploit the sea's resources.

CHAPTER ONE

Contemporary Piracy

Piracy occurs in several parts of the world and, though the phenomenon has a significant international dimension in some cases, it does not currently represent a problem on a global scale.

Definitions

Piracy is, very simply, unlawful depredation at sea. While not politically motivated in itself, it has invariably been linked to prevailing political conditions and the expression of state power or, more commonly, state weakness. This connection has meant that common notions of piracy have rarely been applied uniformly or unambiguously, as activities that are called piracy in one place at one time perform 'legitimate' functions for states at others, as in the case of privateering.

For the British jurist C.S. Kenny, piracy was 'any armed violence at sea which is not a lawful act of war'.[1] Kenny's definition was echoed by J.L. Anderson, who characterised piracy as a 'subset of violent maritime predation in that it is not part of a declared or widely recognised war'.[2] The IMB defines piracy pragmatically as:

> An act of boarding or attempting to board any ship with the intent to commit theft or any other crime and with the intent or capability to use force in the furtherance of that act.[3]

The United Nations Convention on the Law of the Sea of 1982 (UNCLOS), however, is more circumscribed. Article 101 describes piracy as:

a) any illegal acts of violence or detention, or any act of depredation, committed for private ends by the crew or the passengers of a
   private ship or a private aircraft, and directed:
   i   on the high seas, against another ship or aircraft, or against
       persons or property on board such ship or aircraft;
   ii against a ship, aircraft, persons or property in a place outside
       the jurisdiction of any State;
b) any act of voluntary participation in the operation of a ship or of an
   aircraft with knowledge of facts making it a pirate ship or aircraft.[4]

This narrower definition is used by the United Nations' shipping regulator, the International Maritime Organisation (IMO). Because UNCLOS restricts piracy, and thus law-enforcement action against it, to the high seas (the area beyond territorial waters, which extend twelve nautical miles (nm) from the shore), pirates have in many cases evaded capture by sailing from the high seas to the territorial seas of jurisdictions that are ill-equipped to combat maritime crime, thereby putting themselves beyond the reach of international and domestic law. In addition, states typically resent, and therefore try to prevent, entry into their jurisdictions by foreign navies and coast guards, and pirates exploit this by crossing into another country's waters if discovered and pursued by the first state they enter.[5]

The UK's House of Commons Transport Committee in its June 2006 report on piracy observed that 'the absence of a single definition means that the classification of violent maritime incidents can become a matter of dispute and confusion'.[6] Drafters of laws and governments in affected areas have tended to pay scant attention to the difficulties caused by this confusion. By contrast, the naval officers, police and coast guards charged with suppressing piracy almost certainly favour the simpler, broader defi-nition, as do pirates' victims. For them the distinction between an act of piracy, which under current international law can only occur on the 'high seas', and 'armed robbery at sea', which occurs only within territorial waters, is of little relevance.

Reasons for piracy

Piracy is a low-risk criminal activity that pays well. It occurs for one over-riding reason: opportunity. Poverty is often cited as the main motivator, but this is simplistic. Certainly diversions of trade flows away from particular regions have in the past caused affected groups in those regions to resort to piracy; equally today, changes in financial circumstances will encourage some to try their hand, but economic necessity is not a first cause.[7] In most eras and in most places piracy has been dominated by organised gangs that have treated it as a business.[8] Seven major factors enable piracy to flourish:

- Legal and jurisdictional weakness
- Favourable geography
- Conflict and disorder
- Under-funded law enforcement/inadequate security
- Permissive political environments
- Cultural acceptability
- Promise of reward

Legal and jurisdictional weakness
The legal and jurisdictional difficulties that law enforcement agencies face help to reduce the risks run by pirates.[9] The most significant obstacle is state sovereignty; states typically allow external coast guards and police to operate in their waters to counter a common threat only with the greatest reluctance. In some jurisdictions, for instance India and Japan, piracy is not even a crime. In order for the problem of pirate impunity to be overcome, uniform domestic anti-piracy legislation across states needs to be coupled with a demonstrable willingness on the part of all states to prosecute and extradite perpetrators, not simply deport them.

There have been some attempts to tackle this problem. In 1992 the Convention for the Suppression of Unlawful Acts Against the Safety of Maritime Navigation (SUA) came into force, having been signed by 126 countries.While it was designed to deal with politically motivated violence at sea,because it addresses acts such as ship seizure and violence on board and damage to ships and cargo, it could also be applicable to piracy where violence is involved.[10] SUA applies everywhere at sea, including in territorial waters, providing the ship under attack is coming from or proceeding to an international destination. Its provisions state that parties must enact domestic legislation to make convention offences punishable under domestic law. The main aim of the agreement is prosecution, not prevention; its central purpose is to ensure that states either prosecute or extradite. There are, however, limitations to SUA that mean it does not pose a serious challenge to maritime violence: it cannot be invoked if the violence on board is insufficient to compromise maritime safety, and it is not applicable to the intra-state coastal traffic that accounts for so much movement in the territorial and archipelagic waters where the majority of pirate attacks take place. Furthermore, many of the states in Asia where the piracy problem is most acute are not signatories.[11] The result has been that – apart from in one minor case in US waters – SUA has never been invoked.

International law on piracy, in the form of UNCLOS, also has serious limitations:

- The restriction of the definition of piracy to 'private', as opposed to 'public' or 'political' acts, excluding terrorists and insurgents
- The geographical restriction of piracy to the high seas
- The absence of a mechanism to ensure that hot pursuit into a state's territorial waters is not prevented by that state
- The 'two ship requirement' that excludes internal seizure from the definition of piracy
- The absence of a requirement that states enact domestic anti-piracy laws
- The absence of a requirement that states cooperate in anti-piracy measures
- The absence of a mechanism for penalising states' failure to discharge agreed responsibilities in relation to combating piracy
- The absence of a disputes procedure

Favourable geography
Piracy is only sustainable in places that offer a combination of rewarding hunting grounds, moderate levels of risk and proximate safe havens.[12] A popular image of a pirate attack is of a fast ship bearing down on a slow, lonely merchantman on the high seas. In reality, for the most part, piracy has historically taken place close to coasts or in narrow seas such as the Caribbean, the Mediterranean, the English Channel and the South China Sea. This is still the case: contemporary piracy is land-based and concentrated in a limited number of areas, principally Southeast Asia, the Bay of Bengal, Somalia and Tanzania, the West African coast (especially off Nigeria) and parts of South America, in narrow seas and close to the shore.

When ships are under way, attacks generally take place in straits, bays, estuaries and archipelagos, where vessels are forced to move close to shore for navigational or commercial reasons and which therefore offer pirates the best opportunities. Narrow seas are also generally more crowded than the high seas, which means more targets. Crowded seas also force large ships to move slowly, making them easier to board and less able to take evasive action such as fishtailing to destabilise the pirate vessel or speeding up to lose it.

Conflict and disorder

Piracy – and criminality at sea generally – can thrive when coastal regions are troubled by war or civil disturbance, or their aftermath, as the absence of law-enforcing authorities and desperate circumstances combine to draw people towards criminality. Lebanon became a haven for criminal activity during its civil war from 1975 to 1990 and 'unofficial' ports sprang up along the coast to handle stolen cargo and refit stolen ships.[13] Similarly the sundering of Somalia into warring fiefdoms following the collapse of the Siad Barre dictatorship in January 1991 appears to have triggered the country's piracy problem.[14]

Under-funded law enforcement

Inadequate state funding and training of police, coast guards and navies allows pirates the freedom to operate. Many states cannot afford the personnel, equipment or organisational resources needed to tackle the problem successfully, and/or they direct resources towards other priorities, as in the case of Indonesia.[15]

Law enforcement at sea is expensive; there are huge sea areas to be protected. It requires boats well equipped with radar, communications and, most importantly, well-trained and honest crews who have sound knowledge of the local waters and weather. It also requires shore-based command and control facilities with access to dependable information about ship movements and cargoes, and reliable intelligence about pirate activity. To be truly effective, surface search and interdiction also needs air support for surveillance and, if necessary, the deployment of police or marines.

For many states, such levels of security are unsustainable. In 1992, Indonesia, Malaysia and Singapore adopted a policy of aggressively patrolling the Malacca Strait, resulting in the virtual elimination of pirate activity. Despite its success, the policy had to be abandoned after six months because it was so expensive.[16] The Asian financial crisis of the 1990s also meant that regional states were forced to reduce the resources they made available for surveillance. The problem became worse after the 11 September attacks, as attention was focused on security measures on land, leaving countries such as the Philippines and Indonesia with even fewer resources to spend at sea.[17]

Permissive political environment

To flourish, piracy requires lax, as well as under-resourced, law enforce-ment.[18] Such laxity is almost always the consequence of state weakness. In the absence of a hegemonic power, a widespread unwillingness to take action against piracy has formed the typical backdrop to events at sea.

Where permissive environments exist within states and their terri-torial waters, they generally come about either because the political environment is corrupt locally or nationally, or because law enforcement is under-funded. Often, of course, both conditions apply. Where police are underpaid, they typically connive with criminals in order to make a living. Many pirates depend on a supportive criminal infrastructure to supply them with intelligence and equipment and to dispose of stolen goods, even entire cargoes, if necessary. Such an infrastructure can have connections to corrupt law enforcers.[19] The most notorious example of the connivance between the authorities and pirates took place in the Gulf of Thailand after the end of the Vietnam War, when the exploitation of thousands of Vietnamese refugees by pirate gangs took place with, despite the efforts of the UNHCR, the inaction of the world community, and the full knowledge, not only of local police, but of littoral governments.[20]

The chronic piracy problem in Indonesia has been fed by Jakarta's indifference. Elements in the Indonesian police and navy have allegedly been involved in piracy for years, but the central authorities have ignored the problem.[21] On the island of Belakang Padang off the coast of Batam, near Singapore, pirates' identities are well known locally, but the police have no interest in arresting them. On the contrary, they are, according to French maritime security researcher Eric Frécon, 'not only tolerant of the criminal activities of the pirates but [they are] also accomplices and act as bodyguards'.[22]

While every state has the right to arrest pirates on the high seas and arraign them under its own domestic laws, few do. Even a strong state such as the United States has found legal and practical impediments have limited its ability to prosecute pirates. When American forces arrested pirates off the coast of Somalia in 2006, the US was reluctant to try them domestically because of problems gathering evidence and confusion over jurisdiction, and the logistical difficulties of transferring prisoners to a court in the US.

Various attempts have been made to counteract the generalised failure to confront piracy, notably in November 2005, when a dramatic increase in piracy off the coast of Somalia culminated in a major attack on a cruise ship, prompting the IMO to formulate its Resolution A 979 (24), which called on all seafarers and other involved parties to work within international law to ensure that further acts of piracy in the region were prevented and current ones terminated. The resolution was not adopted by the UN Security Council as the IMO had hoped, but it did move the Security Council to issue an anti-piracy statement.[23]

Yet despite interventions such as these, pirates in most regions continue to operate freely, in sharp contrast to the situation 80 or so years ago: in 1925 it was reasonable to assume that piracy had become almost obsolete, due to the ubiquity of the Royal Navy and other naval forces and a forceful response to piracy on the part of the imperial powers over much of the previous century.[24]

Cultural acceptability
Piracy thrives where it is culturally acceptable, an important fact that is often overlooked. Trading patterns are one factor that helps to determine what becomes culturally acceptable – it is likely that a reason for piracy's greater acceptability in Southeast Asia than in West Africa is that rich cargoes have transited Southeast Asian archipelagos for centuries, making the opportunity for piracy a permanent feature of the local environment to an extent that it was not in West Africa. Furthermore, piracy frequently operates on a clan or family basis, as in the Riau-Lingga archipelago in Indonesia, where a tradition has existed for generations.[25]

The promise of reward
Sums that might appear paltry in the developed world make piracy well worth the risks to those involved – there are numerous reports of petty theft at sea, of paint being stolen from lockers and rope from decks. But, as the Organisation for Economic Cooperation and Development (OECD) has observed, piracy can also be 'a highly lucrative venture'.[26] The British criminologist Jon Vagg has analysed the cash takings from 83 pirate attacks in Indonesian waters over the 1991–92 period (there is little reason to believe that, inflation apart, the rewards reaped have changed much since the time of the study). His findings show that in at least 30% of cases, the pirates took more than $1,000, which, even if split between members of a gang, was a good return on a night's activity in a country where the per capita annual income at the time was $638.[27] Swedish academic Stefan Eklöf estimates that in 1997 a gang member operating in the Malacca Strait could expect to take home between $500 and $700 from each attack.[28] One of the reasons why the frequency of pirate attacks on large international carriers may be falling is that large ships now carry much less cash than

they did a decade ago; a direct response to this kind of major theft from ships' safes.[29]

Cash thefts may be supplemented by the sale of portable equipment plus whatever valuables the pirates find on the crew and in their quarters. The RAND Corporation's Peter Chalk, who has written extensively on Asian issues including piracy, has suggested that on this basis the average take from a raid is now around $10,000; similarly, maritime policy analyst Mark J. Valencia has quoted a figure of between $5,000 and $15,000.[30]

Types of ship attacked

Large vessels on international voyages are not pirates' prime targets. There were a number of attacks on such ships during the 1990s, particularly in Southeast Asia, which caught the attention of the international press, but few have taken place more recently, perhaps because large ships now pass through known pirate areas on high alert and with less cash on board. A study of attacks in the Malacca Strait between 2000 and 2005 showed an overall reduction in assaults on ships above 20,000 gross registered tonnes (GRT).[31] Nonetheless, large ships remain vulnerable, due to the trend towards reducing crew sizes that began in the 1960s and accelerated dramatically in the late 1970s and early 1980s as a result of containerisation, automation and downward pressures on cost. Smaller crews mean more work and higher levels of fatigue for those who remain.[32] Pirates in the Malacca and Singapore Straits and elsewhere in the region appear to favour bulk carriers among large ships, probably because they have low freeboards,[33] as well as minimal crews.

But pirates on the whole prefer to attack smaller vessels. The crews of smaller ships also tend to be more at risk of being kidnapped; during the period of the study of attacks in the Malacca Strait, only five abductions took place on vessels of more than 1,000 GRT, compared to 26 on smaller vessels.[34] The study also highlighted the fact that most attacks are on local craft rather than on vessels engaged in international trade.[35]

Methods of boarding and attack

Ships stationary in ports, harbours or anchorages are usually pirates' favoured targets, mainly because they are the easiest to board. Mark Farley, a lieutenant commander in the US Navy who conducted an analysis of Office of Naval Intelligence (ONI) data on piracy from 1989 to 1993, found that stationary ships (of all sizes) were boarded successfully in more than 90% of cases, but this figure dropped to 62% when ships were under way.[36] Traditionally, the most common method used against ships under way is to approach the stern with a fast boat at night. Although this appears still to be the most commonly used technique in Southeast Asia, even here it has been replaced on occasion, as it has been elsewhere, by the use of multiple fast-moving boats to weave in front of and around a target to distract the bridge while accomplices board at the back (a consequence of the wider availability of powerful outboard motors) and by the use of actual or threatened gunfire aimed at the bridge or wheelhouse to force vessels to stop and lower a ladder.[37] The availability of cheap weapons such as AK-47 automatic rifles and rocket-propelled grenades has substantially increased the threat pirates are able to pose even to large ships. Cheap and powerful outboard motors have greatly facilitated pirate operations, lengthening the time pirates can spend in target areas by reducing transit times and giving them the speed to catch and hold station with large ships, and the endurance to sustain an attack for several hours if necessary.

As the technology available to pirates improves, the shipping industry is often accused of not doing enough to protect its own assets. Vessels typically take basic precautions in pirate-prone areas, such as standing extra watches, priming fire hoses so they are ready to be used to douse suspicious small craft if they come too close, and fitting locks to doors to create 'citadels' where the crew can ride out attacks. While sophisticated equipment such as electronic tracking devices and high-voltage fences installed outboard the ship's rail might be affordable for large shipping companies, it is far too expensive for the operators of the small ships that are most commonly attacked. The alternative is to allow ships' crews to exercise their right of self-defence, using firearms. This is an unpopular option, however, due to the risk of escalation.[38] Many states place severe restrictions on what arms, if any, can be carried at sea, and the International Ship and Port Facility Security Code demands that any arms on board be declared on entering a port.

The cost of piracy

No systematic study of the cost of piracy has been undertaken.[39] Because the impunity of much piracy makes accurate records of losses difficult to gather, estimates vary enormously and analysts often do not disclose what is included in a given calculation. Alan Chan, the managing director of the Singapore-based shipping company Petroships, which owned the merchant vessel *Petro Ranger* that was hijacked in 1998 on its way to Vietnam from Singapore, believes piracy costs the shipping industry roughly $500 million each year in higher insurance premiums, delays and on-board security.[40] Peter Chalk has put the cost at least $1 billion a year.[41]

John Burnett, journalist and author of the 2002 account of modern piracy *Dangerous Waters*, cites the estimate of US–Southeast Asia relations analyst John Brandon that financial losses from maritime crime come to as much as $16bn.[42] Naval strategy researcher Vijay Sakhuja has suggested that piracy costs the world economy around $25bn.[43] By way of comparison with these admittedly highly divergent figures, estimated annual losses from land-based cargo theft worldwide (mostly from trucks) range from $30bn to $50bn.[44] One reason for the substantial variations among the figures for losses to piracy is that analysts disagree over what to include under losses: raised insurance premiums, increased freight rates and money lost to reroutings, for instance, are only counted by some.[45]

Even if the largest of these estimates is accurate, and it is likely that the highest of these figures is much too high, the sums are small when viewed alongside a total worldwide annual maritime commerce figure for 2005 of around $7.8 trillion.[46] To cite an example of a region with signifi-cant pirate activity, the value of the trade that passes through the Malacca Strait each year has been put at well over $500bn, and is probably nearing $2tr.[47] Taking the worst recent year for piracy, 2000, when 75 attacks were reported in the strait, Stefan Eklöf has calculated – assuming an average take from an attack of $5,000, and doubling the number of attacks to allow for unreported cases – a total loss of only $750,000. He points out that this is between 0.001 and 0.002% of the value of the goods transported through the strait.[48] Even if we assume, with Chalk and Valencia, a much higher average take of $10,000, the total loss would still be only $1.5m. As Jack Gottschalk and Brian Flanagan remark in their book on modern piracy, so long as losses remain negligible 'businesses engaged in maritime commerce will have little incentive to take the steps necessary to eradicate, or even to seriously combat, the piracy problem'.[49]

For states that harbour pirates, however unwillingly, costs theoretically include loss of reputation, loss of harbour fees from bunkering services and cruise ship visits, more expensive law enforcement, and environmen-tal damage. However, the commercial costs among these are not currently serious concerns: in modern times 'no known trade has ceased or been re-routed' as a result of piracy.[50]

The IMB is reluctant to put a price on piracy as, in its view, this would detract from the importance of the danger it poses to crews.[51] Seafarers are in theory afforded protection by their own governments and the govern-ments through whose waters they sail. Yet according to Andrew Linnington of the British maritime union NUMAST (now merged with its Dutch equiv-alent to become Nautilus), from 1995 to the middle of 2006, 3,284 seafarers were held hostage, 617 were threatened on board ship, 463 were injured, 349 were killed, 208 suffered actual assault, 112 were kidnapped or held to ransom and 164 are missing presumed dead.[52] Furthermore, many seafarers who have been attacked are too traumatised to return to sea.[53] It must never be forgotten that the cost of piracy is not only economic.

Enumerating pirate attacks

The IMB, which was established by the International Chamber of Commerce in 1979 to combat maritime fraud, receives reports directly from ships or the owners of ships that have been attacked or suspect that they have been targeted for attack, and issues its weekly incident report on the basis of these, as well as a quarterly and annual report.[54] It neither conducts nor tracks subsequent investigations of incidents. The other organisations that publish regular reports on pirate activity are the IMO, which issues monthly reports, quarterly summaries and an annual summary;[55] the UK's Defence Intelligence Staff (DIS), which issues a monthly report; and the ONI, which feeds its information into the US National Geospatial Intelligence Agency's Anti-Shipping Activity Message database.[56] The IMO, DIS and ONI all rely primarily on the IMB for incident reports. In 1992, the IMB established the Piracy Reporting Centre (PRC) in Kuala Lumpur in Malaysia in response to an increasing number of pirate attacks in Southeast Asia. This has become the internationally recognised collection point for piracy reports and statistics. In addition, a new reporting centre, the Information Sharing Centre (ISC), opened in Singapore in December 2006.

There was little recording of pirate attacks before the early 1990s. The IMB has reports dating back to the early 1970s, but it was only in 1984 that the IMO began recording attacks systematically, having noted 'with great concern the increasing number of incidents involving piracy and armed robbery' the previous year.[57] Although the earlier figures are now available, the IMO has only published its piracy statistics since 1995.

What the figures show is that the problem was insignificant throughout the 1980s, increased somewhat in the early 1990s and then increased further from around 1995, with a peak in 2000, after which it declined again somewhat, but remained above the 1990s average (see Figures 2 and 3).

Comprehensive records have been kept for too short a period of time for it to be possible to determine clear long-term trends, but within these limitations, we can point to a growth in incidents, even though this growth is considerably less dramatic than some recent discourse about the inexorable rise of piracy might indicate. Moreover, however sophisticated

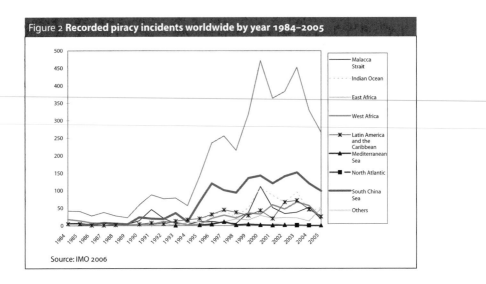

Figure 2 **Recorded piracy incidents worldwide by year 1984–2005**

Source: IMO 2006

Figure 3 **Recorded actual and attempted pirate attacks worldwide by year 1995–2005**

1995	1996	1997	1998	1999	2000	2001	2002	2003	2004	2005	Total
188	228	247	202	300	469	335	370	445	329	276	3,389

Source: IMB 2006

the statistical analyses attempted, the multiple factors affecting piracy make it impossible to confidently predict future trends.

Problems with piracy statistics

The raw data have their limitations, which are discussed in more detail below. To begin with, many incidents of piracy and robbery at sea are not recorded at all. Also, there is disagreement between the major maritime organisations about whether or not attacks on ships at berth and at anchor constitute acts of piracy. The data on regional variation are not satisfactory, as the divisions used are too broad – the IMB records by country and aggregates by region, and the IMO only records by large region, e.g. 'West Africa', making close-up analysis of the figures difficult.

Accuracy

There can be little certainty attached to existing statistics on piracy. One problem is that because the PRC, the source of the most thorough recent data, was established in Southeast Asia in response to what was seen at the time as largely an Asian problem, incidents in other regions were probably under-represented in its first years, thereby skewing some of the early statistics. A more fundamental difficulty is that the IMB depends for its incident reports on ship owners and ships' masters, who choose whether or not to report incidents. Some observers view the IMB's figures with suspicion, because they suspect that victims might exaggerate incidents.[58] But it may well be that dependence on victims' reporting has the opposite effect. For example, from January to September 2006, the IMB recorded only eight attacks in the Malacca Strait, while the Indonesian navy recorded 23 over the same period.[59]

It is widely suspected that under-reporting hides the full extent of the piracy problem. In 1998, the DIS estimated that the number of incidents could be three times the number reported. In the same year, the Australian Defence Intelligence Organisation reported that the number of reported incidents was between 20% and 70% below the total number of incidents.[60] In 1999, Japanese NGO the Nippon Foundation, in its survey of attacks on Japanese shipping in the Malacca Strait, suggested that the number of attacks might be *ten times* the level reported.[61] More recently, the IMB, in its own comment on the figures for 2005, stated 'though the attack numbers have dropped, the IMB would like to stress that many actual and attempted cases also go unreported'.[62] Maritime policy expert Sam Bateman nuances this picture by suggesting that increases in the number of piracy incidents in the recent past may have been overestimated because, as with any crime, incidents went unreported in the past, thereby artificially reducing earlier figures. He contends that under-reporting may in fact be waning as seafarers become more aware that records are kept that acknowledge and monitor the problem.[63]

There is widespread agreement, however, on the reasons for under- and mis-reporting: sometimes the witnesses are dead;[64] in cases involving kidnappings in particular, victims are intimidated into silence; and states and ports, wary of being seen as having a piracy problem, fail to record or report incidents. For shipping companies, there are a variety of motives for keeping quiet: to avoid damaging their reputations (including through the exposure of insufficient precautions taken), to prevent crew demands for additional pay for sailing into or through pirate-prone areas, and to avoid the expense incurred by ships' delay during an investigation (which in several jurisdictions cannot be relied upon to be competent and transparent in any case). According to erstwhile head of the PRC John Martin, several shipping associations have gone as far as to write into their manuals of procedure that ship attacks should not be reported at all.[65]

Some observers have suggested that the ISC in Asia might reduce dependence on IMB incident reports. The ISC was opened as a result of the ratification of the Regional Cooperation Agreement on Combating Piracy and Armed Robbery Against Ships in Asia (ReCAAP) in June 2006.[66] It gathers and collates regional piracy statistics, providing greater detail on incidents than the IMB, follows up on incident reports, and records and monitors the law enforcement response.[67] Each ReCAAP signatory has its own designated point of contact, which receives incident reports and transmits them to the ISC. The ISC regards itself as having a coordination and enforcement role that distinguishes it from the IMB. But doubts have been raised about how effective it will prove to be, not least because it is necessarily as reliant on incident reporting as is the IMB (and, indeed, appears to make considerable use of the IMB's own incident reports).

Because of their reluctance to allow external agencies to operate in their sovereign waters, neither Malaysia nor Indonesia are yet signatories to ReCAAP, nor are likely to be in the near future, and it is difficult to see how the centre will be able to operate effectively without them, given that the bulk of the incidents occur in their waters.[68] Another difficulty is that, as the organisation is under the influence of the participating governments, unwelcome reports showing, for instance, thriving piracy in the waters of a participating state could be suppressed, and statistics may become vulnerable to political influence. There are concerns that, if an incident is reported locally, the national reporting office may not pass it on to the centre. Local and national unwillingness to be branded an area with a pirate problem could well result in the erratic delivery of information about incidents.

There are already signs of confusion within the system. Some captains report incidents to both the ISC and the IMB, and because of time delays this has meant some of the same incidents have been reported as occurring at different times and in different locations. As some captains now report only to the ISC and not to the IMB, the two organisations' statistics do not tally and further uncertainty is introduced into the figures.

Location of ships when attacked
Of the 239 actual and attempted pirate attacks recorded by the IMB in 2006, nearly 63% took place when ships were berthed (15) or at anchor (150).[69] For the IMO, these attacks are not incidences of piracy but, in accordance with the UNCLOS definition, armed robberies against ships. The IMB is unwilling to concede this distinction between piracy and armed robbery at sea. Despite the problems with the narrower definition of piracy, there is a case for separating attacks on berthed ships from piracy elsewhere: these are effectively 'port crimes', perpetrated mainly by the same gangs that steal from warehouses and containers. There is concern in some quarters

that their designation as piracy could divert police attention from the more serious and more often violent crimes that tend to be committed when ships are anchored awaiting a berth or under way at sea, where it is easier to evade capture and pirates therefore have more time at their disposal. In any event, the disagreement over the issue does not aid accurate data collection.

Regional variations and trends

Total numbers of incidents worldwide, as reported by the media, have little real significance because, while piracy occurs in many parts of the world, it does not affect all regions evenly. The best perspective is obtained by looking at the problem at a local and regional level.

Globally, reported piracy may have increased slightly over the decade from 1995 to 2005, peaking in the middle of the period, but variations in the number of attacks in particular regions over the same period have been more dramatic than the global picture shows. For instance, Somali piracy emerged very suddenly to become one of the most serious pirate problems in the world.

In Bangladesh, South America and West Africa, piracy tends to be concentrated around specific ports and localities; in Bangladesh it is mostly in evidence around Chittagong, and the estuarial region in the southwest, which is rarely reported outside the local media; in South America in the ports of Rio de Janeiro and Santos in Brazil, at particular points along the continent's north coast from Surinam to Venezuela, and off Peru; in West Africa it is be found principally in and around Nigeria; off Lagos and in the Bonny River.

The regions that have been troubled most by piracy in recent years and which are therefore worth examining in more detail are Southeast Asia and Somalia.

Case Study 1:

Southeast Asia

The geography of Southeast Asia provides an ideal environment for piracy, and the region's pirate traditions go back virtually uninterrupted to the fifth century BC. A British traveller writing more than a century ago observed that: 'as surely as spiders abound where there are nooks and corners, so have pirates sprung up wherever there is a nest of islands'.[70] More incidents are reported in this region than anywhere else. Pirates can escape easily amongst the maze of islands, reefs, shifting shoals and sand-bars that require intimate knowledge to be safely navigated. They can hide in the creeks, small rivers and mangrove swamps that puncture the coast, and amongst the thousands of other small craft that ply between islands: estimates suggest that the Malacca Strait is crossed by 80,000 people and fished by 10,000 boats daily.[71]

The will to suppress piracy varies significantly among the states of the region: Indonesia, where more pirate incidents take place than in any other country, has traditionally displayed the least interest in its suppression.[72] Cultural acceptance is widespread: in parts of Indonesia and the Philippines, pirates can in many cases mix with the local population without fear of betrayal, due to societal acquiescence in pirate activity.[73] Southeast Asia is, moreover, a region where the piracy phenomenon has regional scope: pirates can easily cross maritime boundaries – some of which are still disputed – to throw off their pursuers. They may hijack a ship in the waters of one state and dispose of its cargo in another, while the men controlling the operation are often based in a third state.

Indonesia

Indonesia is a country intertwined with many narrow seas. It covers a vast area, large parts of which lie beyond the writ of central government, and claims a coastline of 81,000km, approximately twice the circumference of the Earth. Even its government is not sure how many islands make up the archipelago.[74] Although the state is concerned about maritime security generally, issues other than piracy have tended to receive more attention in Jakarta, with piracy against ships transiting Indonesian waters an especially low priority.[75] Smuggling of people and goods, and the degradation of the maritime environment by over-fishing, are of most concern to the government, with some reason: in 2002, it estimated that illegal fishing was costing the country more than $4bn annually.[76] Such competing problems and priorities help to explain why Indonesia's position at the top of the list of countries experiencing pirate activity has remained unchallenged since 1991, though there have been some improvements, including increased participation in regional security initiatives.

The Philippines

Until recently, the Philippines appeared to be developing a piracy problem on a similar scale to Indonesia's, but in 2004 it suffered only four reported attacks, allegedly none in 2005 and six in 2006. This apparent decline may be due to under-reporting, rather than a real fall in incidents, as the Philippines is as troubled by corruption and poorly funded law enforcement as is Indonesia. Under-reporting has been a problem in the Philippines in the past. According to Eric Ellen, the then director-general of the IMB, there were 143 cases of piracy in Philippine waters in 1993, none of which were reported, and according to the Philippine navy and coast guard, there were 1,329 pirate attacks between 1993 and 2005, making the supposed decline from 2004 dramatic indeed.[77] The armed forces and law enforcement agencies of both the Philippines and Indonesia are struggling to control maritime crime, regardless of official statements to the contrary.[78]

The Malacca and Singapore Straits
The picture in the straits between Singapore, Malaysia and Indonesia is clearer. Because such a large proportion of the world's trade passes through these straits, pirate events there tend to be subject to greater political and media attention than elsewhere, and there is more information about them available. Piracy in the straits is characterised by its variety. According to the provincial head of operations of the Indonesian Marine Police, three types of pirate were operating in Indonesia's Riau Islands near the straits in 2005: the first comprised small gangs of robbers earning a meagre living from ad hoc petty theft; the second, based on Batam, went after tug boats to hijack then sell; the third was armed, highly organised and targeted larger ships, especially tankers with foreign flags.[79]

Because the straits are narrow and crowded, attacks by all three types have been perpetrated in or close to international shipping lanes, raising concerns that pirates might affect the flow of international trade. But the probability of an international carrier suffering a pirate attack in the straits is extremely low: Stefan Eklöf has calculated that, based on 200 ship transits a day in 2004 (this figure excludes intra-strait traffic), the probability of an attack on any one vessel was less than 0.2%.[80] A study by Sam Bateman and his colleagues estimated that from 2000 to 2005, the proportion of vessels attacked represented between 0.06% and 0.19% of the total traffic in the straits, and that most of the ships targeted had been travelling between local ports.[81]

But despite the low probability of a pirate attack, the geography of the strait means that an attack could potentially have wider implications than for the targeted vessel alone: many attacks are on vessels under way in congested waters, where sudden changes in the weather and in the sea itself, such as shifting sandbanks, mean that crews must exercise great care and attention for ships to be navigated safely. If a large ship or one carrying a hazardous cargo were left without bridge control during a pirate attack, it could collide with another vessel (as apparently happened between the oil tanker *Nagasaki Spirit* and the container ship *Ocean Blessing* in 1992, causing an oil spill and a major fire[82]) or run aground, blocking or polluting a key channel.

Reported pirate activity in the straits has declined somewhat in recent years. The straits, which together suffered 80 attacks in 2000, recorded only 19 in 2005. Although the reasons for this are not clear, three factors seem to be at work: greater national and regional counter-piracy activity, following many years of Japanese encouragement in that direction and the 2004 US proposal for a cooperative maritime security arrangement among regional states, or Regional Maritime Security Initiative, which, though never put into practice because of the opposition of those states wary of superpower involvement in their affairs, was nonetheless the catalyst for greater cooperation between them; the effects on Aceh of the 2004 tsunami, which severely damaged pirate communities and resources; and the more decisive law-enforcement actions of Prime Minister Abdullah Badawi's government in Malaysia compared to those of his predecessor, Mahathir Mohamad, whose intense nationalism had undermined anti-piracy co-operation with other countries.

New security measures, including airborne patrols, were introduced by the littoral states in late 2005.[83] Whether because of these and other multilateral arrangements such as the Indonesian–Malaysian–Singaporean 'MALSINDO' patrols, begun in 2004, there were no attacks in the early months of 2006, and some maritime security observers in the region and internationally expressed the hope that the problem had been eliminated, though others were more cautious.[84] But attacks resumed in April 2006, and had reached a total of 16 by the year's end.[85] Moreover, attacks on fishing vessels, which rarely feature in the international statistics, have, according to Malaysian maritime security analyst J.N. Mak and others, continued unabated.[86] The fall in pirate activity has not, therefore, been nearly as dramatic as some analysts initially thought.[87] The frequency of attacks on international shipping in the straits may have declined slightly, but few perpetrators have been caught and, given the persistent character of the problem, it is quite possible that the gangs are biding their time until the current crackdown ends.[88]

Case Study 2:

Somalia

Outside Asia, it is in the waters around the Horn of Africa that the pirate presence has been greatest over the past few years. The problem began in the region in the early 1990s as an aspect of the generalised disorder that followed the overthrow of the socialist dictator Muhammad Siad Barre by clan-based warlords, although its precise origins are unclear. In 1995, the IMO reported the case of MV *Bonsella*, which was attacked in September 1994 by a party of 26 pirates posing as coast guards who for six days used it as a base from which to attack other ships.[89] By 1998, two-thirds of all maritime abductions worldwide were taking place in the Gulf of Aden, close to Somalia.[90]

In 2000, there were 23 incidents of piracy recorded in the Red Sea–Aden–Somalia region, a third of the African total.[91] This level was sustained throughout 2001. The number of reported piracy incidents then declined over the following three years – in 2004, only ten were recorded. It is possible that the arrival in 2001 of the US-assembled multinational Coalition Task Force (CTF) 150 to patrol the seas between Pakistan and Somalia, mustered with the purpose of finding escaping high-ranking members of al-Qaeda, contributed to the decline. But the interval was brief. In 2005, pirate attacks had resumed in earnest off the Somali coast, aided by continuing warlord-ism on land.

In November 2005 the Bahamas-flagged, US-operated cruise liner *Seabourn Spirit*, sailing about 100 miles off the coast, well within the area that the IMB and ONI advised ships to avoid, was attacked and chased by a group of pirates firing automatic rifles and rocket-propelled grenades.[92] It managed to increase speed and escape but the incident drew the world media's attention to the issue of Somali piracy. The attack, as an assault on a passenger ship under US ownership and as such an object of international attention, was the prompt for the IMO's appeal to the UN on the issue. The Security Council's March 2006 response stated that member states with naval vessels active in the region should be vigilant to piracy and 'take appropriate action to protect merchant shipping, in particular the transportation of humanitarian aid, against any such act, in line with relevant international law … The Council further urges cooperation among all States, particularly regional states, and active prosecution of piracy offences.'[93]

The US government also took a more serious view of the piracy problem in the Horn of Africa after the incident, and the US Navy, with the support of its Coalition partners, adopted an aggressive posture towards the problem and instituted more regular and thorough patrols along the Somali coast, resulting in two interdictions of pirate craft in 2006. This discouraged pirates from entering international shipping lanes and restricted their activities to coastal waters for a time, though pirate attacks continued through the first half of 2006.

In May and June 2006, the warlords' rule collapsed and the Islamist-influenced Islamic Courts Union (ICU)[94] established control in several towns, including Mogadishu. The ICU successfully suppressed the pirates, who had operated under the protection and possible direction of the warlords, by shutting down their bases. US-backed Ethiopian forces, however, defeated the ICU in December 2006 and removed it from power. Following the collapse of ICU rule, there were signs that pirate activity was resuming. In December 2006, the ONI reported that a cargo ship, the *Sheila McDevitt*, had encountered a suspected pirate vessel 120 miles off the coast the previous month,[95] and early in 2007, there was a report that pirates were re-assembling at Xarardheere, the east-coast town that had been the base for the pirate group that had been the most active prior to the ICU takeover. In February 2007 a small cargo ship, the MV *Rozen*, was hijacked and its crew held for ransom off the coast of Puntland in northeast Somalia as it returned from delivering World Food Programme relief supplies and another cargo ship, the MV *Nimattulah*, was hijacked on 1 April 2007 off Mogadishu and taken to Dhighily in Puntland.[96] Reports issued in May 2007 indicate that pirate activity has resumed in the shipping lanes, with an attack recorded 200nm from the coast.[97]

Somali piracy appears to be a hybrid of common and organised pirate types. At sea Somali pirates have tended in general to employ basic methods and haphazard planning but the tactic of hijacking vessels and holding them, along with crew and cargo, to ransom is a relatively sophisticated and more organised aspect of their operations.[98] The lawless conditions in Somalia mean that it is possible to moor a ship beyond the reach of rescue or retaliation, making it an ideal place for ransom-based piracy to thrive. The ransom income of Somali pirates can be substantial: the Xarardheere-based gang, the 'Somali Marines', apparently demanded $1m and eventually settled for $800,000 for the return of the *Dongwon-ho*, a South Korean tuna-fishing vessel they captured in April 2006.

During the brief period in which it was active, from 2004 to 2006, the Somali Marines stood out among the region's pirates in its willingness to venture far out to sea. In 2004, the IMB was advising ships to sail at least 50nm (93km) from the Somali coast, preferably further, but by autumn 2005 it had revised this to 150nm.[99] Even these distances did not appear to be far enough. In November 2005, a general cargo vessel reported that it was chased for an hour and a half 390 miles out to sea.[100] Despite the warnings, ships continued to sail closer to the coast than advisable, and it is believed that the Somali Marines were responsible for the attack on the *Seabourn Spirit*, among several others.

However, their success in locating targets far out to sea, and the sophistication of Somali pirate gangs' activities in general, should not be exaggerated. Some attempted attacks reported to have taken place 200nm or more from the coast – including the supposed chase at 390 miles – could have been cases of masters, fearing a pirate attack, confusing at a distance the sight of a fishing ship deploying its nets with a mother ship preparing to deploy fast boats.

Much Somali piracy appears to have its roots in fishing disputes: the absence of any effective authority operating along Africa's longest national coastline has meant that fishing vessels from Europe and East Asia have been able to exploit the area's rich marine resources at the expense of locals, causing dangerous tensions.[101] Some commentators argue that the main sources of piracy in the region are the armed groups formed by local fishermen in response to unregulated fishing, that subsequently become pirate gangs.[102] Certainly the issue is cited by those accused of piracy: the Somalis captured by the US Navy ship USS *Gonzalez* in March 2006 apparently claimed to be defending local fishermen by 'taxing' illicit foreign trawlers, as did the attackers of the *Dongwon-ho* the following month.[103]

Pirate typology and risk assessment

In 1993 an IMO working group concluded that piracy in the Malacca Strait region could be divided into three categories and that these categories were also applicable elsewhere:

- Low-level armed robbery: opportunistic attacks mounted close to land
- Medium-level armed assault and robbery: piracy carried out further from shore, often in narrow sea lanes, with a high probability that violence will be used
- Major criminal hijack: well-resourced and smoothly run operations in which violence is commonly employed not only to steal money or cargo from a ship but also to take over the ship itself[104]

This typology is not entirely satisfactory, despite its popularity among analysts. It focuses too closely on the maritime context of piracy, and the methods and immediate consequences of attacks at sea. Clearly, piracy has its most visible effects at sea, and pirate activity compromises maritime safety and security. It is, however, as much a land-based activity as a maritime one. Its origins are on land, its bases and its markets are on land, and some of its effects are felt on land, principal among them its contribution to corruption. The degree to which piracy affects communities on land, though, does depend on the degree to which it is an organised activity with links to other organised crime or corrupt networks within legitimate authorities.

Anderson offers a more satisfactory categorisation from an historical perspective. He sees three types, based on what he calls piracy's 'form' or 'expression': parasitic, which feeds on successful maritime trade or wealthy littorals; episodic, which arises at specific moments as the result of the weakening of imperial or state power and the consequent distortion in trading patterns, whereby communities abruptly lose income sources they have relied on at the same time as the imperial power withdraws its law enforcers; and intrinsic, in which piracy is a component part of a society's fiscal or commercial life.[105] Applying these categories today, he reaches the balanced judgement that 'piracy committed on commercial shipping, although perhaps organised by criminal groups and essentially parasitic, can have an element of intrinsic predation', because pirates and their vessels are able to blend into local shipping, and local communities may 'knowingly give them shelter and support'.[106] This is an accurate assessment of piracy emanating from many peripheral coastal communities in Southeast Asia.

However, when addressing the problem of contemporary piracy in terms of its potential impact on international security, a more flexible typology has greater practical application. When evaluating how much piracy represents a threat to *security,* as opposed to maritime safety, in a particular country or region, or internationally via that country or region, two assessments must be made. The first is an assessment of the country or region's vulnerability. The second is an assessment of the threat posed. Generally speaking, threat increases the more organised pirate activity becomes. Vulnerability, therefore, must be measured against the degree of pirate organisation in order for a risk assessment to be made for a given area. Organisational capacity can be assessed on a scale that ranges from common criminal piracy to highly organised criminal piracy.

At present, assessments of this kind are undertaken by a number of governmental and commercial bodies in different parts of the world. Affected parties accord different weight to various aspects of the problem according to their own priorities, but because the attitude and policies of states are key to any response, it is the damage piracy may inflict on governments' reputations or political standing that is likely to have the most influence on policy. Since 2001, real or suspected links between piracy and terrorism have tended to overshadow all other threats posed by pirate activity in risk assessments.

Vulnerability assessment

Vulnerability can be difficult to assess, and mistakes are often made. Geographical and environmental features such as weather patterns and the width and depth of shipping channels are generally familiar, and their effects on a region's susceptibility to piracy, and the extent to which piracy has consequences for its security, can more or less be calculated. However, the effects of human factors such as corruption and low morale among law enforcers and other officials are notoriously harder to judge. Even if a coast guard has sophisticated anti-piracy equipment at its disposal, for instance, crews may not be sufficiently motivated to work effectively because they are underpaid. The precise effects of this kind of handicap are difficult to measure. Furthermore, differences in culture and political priorities can mean that interest groups – littoral and user states, shipping companies and their insurers, for example – view the same natural and societal conditions very differently. In practice, therefore, any assessment will usually represent a compromise view.

Conditions that make a littoral state vulnerable to piracy in a way that could impact on security beyond its borders are shown in Figure 4. Once a piracy problem extends its reach beyond the littoral state, diplomatic issues come into play. Problems can arise when an issue of piracy moves from being a security concern shared among states to being the focus of a security dispute among those states, an example being the pirate attacks on the Vietnamese boat people, which caused tensions among Malaysia, Thailand and Vietnam and between these countries and the international community.

Threat assessment

Threat is also difficult to measure, though perhaps less so than vulnerability. Piracy patterns in particular areas, even the capabilities of particular groups, are often known. What are usually less well understood are the connections that groups may have to wider networks of organised crime, politicians, officials and, sometimes, insurgents or terrorists, and how these are likely to influence the groups' activities and reach. Nonetheless, a general principle stands that as the capabilities of a gang increase or criminality in an area becomes more organised, so the threat presented to *international* interests is likely to become more substantial. A highly organised gang is able to pursue larger and more significant targets, such as oil

Figure 4 **Local conditions that make piracy a potential problem beyond the borders of a littoral state**	
Waterways and trade routes:	International traffic volume
	Vulnerable to interruption
	Absence of alternative routes
Type of maritime traffic:	Oil and gas
	Nuclear materials
	Naval and military movements
Littoral state characteristics:	Inadequate navigation aids and maritime safety capability
	Low state stability
	Inadequate security/law enforcement capacity
	Low integrity of criminal justice system
	High local tolerance of pirate activity (cultural acceptability)
	Criminal influence over government organisations
	Limited international security/justice cooperation

tankers, and dispose of their cargoes, with consequently greater potential financial and social impact, than can less organised gangs. It is usually able to do so because of the connections it has to wider criminal networks and corrupt elements in officialdom. Ultimately such pirate activity can undermine the stability of a vulnerable state both through the corruption it feeds and through the fiscal strain imposed by the need for larger and better-equipped security forces. Such instability potentially presents a risk to regional security, and has international security implications in commercial hubs and in regions with valuable resources such as oil, minerals and even fish. Figure 5 indicates characteristic patterns of organised piracy (i.e. gangs who undertake planned operations, often with the help of wider criminal networks) and ad hoc, or 'common', piracy, and gives a sense of the contexts in which each pirate type will tend to operate.

Attack location
Common criminal pirate activity takes place close to coasts, in the main when ships are stationary in port or anchored just offshore. Most attacks by organised pirates, by contrast, takes place outside ports, most often in international waters.

Target identification
In the vast majority of cases, common pirates put to sea on the lookout for small vessels and opportunistically attack ones with low freeboards, those that have taken insufficient anti-piracy measures, or fishing craft. Organised pirates, on the other hand, target specific ships in advance and usually have a buyer waiting for the cargo. Peter Chalk suggests that

Figure 5 **Features of common and organised piracy**		
Characteristics of pirate operations	**Common criminal piracy (lesser threat to international security)**	**Organised criminal piracy (greater threat to international security)**
Attack location:		
Ports and harbours	*	
Anchorages	*	
Coastal waters	*	*
High seas		*
Target identification:		
Opportunity	*	
Intelligence-based planning		*
Target interception:		
Direct	*	
Deception		*
'Sleeper' (infiltrator on board)		*
Attack duration:		
Long	*	
Short		*
Focus of operations:		
Cash theft	*	
Theft of crew belongings	*	
Theft of small craft, inc. yachts	*	Specialised
Theft of cargo		*
Theft of ships		*
Theft of ship + cargo		*
Kidnap-and-ransom		*
'Phantom ship' fraud		*
Violence:		
Propensity to use or threaten	Mid to high	High
Posing threat to environment	*	
Markets:		
Access to local	*	*
Access to international		*
Links to insurgent/terrorist groups:	Most unlikely	Possible but unlikely
Level of official support:		
Low-level or none	*	
Moderate/high		*
Links to organised crime:		
None to occasional	*	
Frequent to integrated		*

such groups rely on intelligence on cargoes, ships, routes and buyers, and government counter-measures, from brokers in several countries.[107]

Target interception

Common pirates attack their targets either overtly, for instance using fire-arms to persuade a target to heave to, or more usually covertly, by boarding the target ship surreptitiously. Organised pirates may in addition employ deception techniques, such as disguising their boats and themselves as police, coast guards or naval personnel. This can be especially effective if they *are* indeed members of such services, as they sometimes are. In Southeast Asia, organised pirates have been known to place a sleeper aboard a target vessel, to transmit updates of the ship's position and help the gang get on board.[108]

Attack persistence

Common and organised pirates often press their attacks with equal vigour. Ships currently have a number of non-violent methods they can employ to discourage boarding: speed, manoeuvre, fishtailing, the use of powerful lights, noise and high-pressure water jets. Persistence, however, motivated by the belief that a victim can be terrified or exhausted into stopping, is likely to be an indicator of common criminal piracy. Some ships have been chased and harried for hours. Organised pirates are more likely to be able to mount their attack quickly and effectively, because they will tend to have intelligence on a ship's course and defensive capabilities, have the resources to mount more effective deceptions, employ heavier firearms and be able to place a sleeper on board.

Focus of operations

Common pirates usually take cash, personal belongings and items of a ship's equipment, then depart. Organised pirates will also take cash and anything else that comes to hand, but their main purpose is either to steal the cargo by stealing the entire vessel, to kidnap members of the crew, or hijack ships and their crews together for combined ransoms.

Organised piracy seeks substantial profits. These can be earned in three ways: ship and cargo theft, cargo fraud, and kidnap-and-ransom (K&R). Ship and cargo theft is when a ship is hijacked with its cargo and, after being disguised and re-registered, is sailed to a port where the cargo is sold. The ship may then be sold to an unsuspecting buyer or, in some cases, for scrap:[109] small vessels are taken to remote bays or harbours where the cargo is offloaded and the ship cut up. Larger ships may be stripped of their components, while ships of all sizes may simply be abandoned. One of the first recorded instances of ship and cargo theft took place in 1990 with the hijacking of the *Marta*, sailing from Thailand to Korea. The most notorious cases have been those of the *Anna Sierra*, hijacked off Thailand in 1995, the *Cheung Son*, attacked near Hong Kong in 1998, and the *Alondra Rainbow*, hijacked on its way from Indonesia to Japan in 1999.[110] Improved security measures and greater awareness of the problem amongst harbour authorities and shippers has meant the gangs involved in this form of theft have had to become more ingenious. On 10 July 2006, the MV *Kimtrans Mega-Lift* left Pangkalbalam, Indonesia for Singapore loaded with about 800 tonnes of tin ingots; on 12 July the ship was hijacked and crew abandoned in a small boat; the following day the ship was seen sinking. Reports indicate that pirates had intentionally sunk the vessel in shallow water to hide it from authorities and so that they could later dive and salvage the valuable cargo. Such activities can only be undertaken by a gang with considerable technical knowledge.[111]

Cargo fraud takes several forms. Only one is related to piracy directly: the 'phantom ship' scam, whereby stolen (usually hijacked) vessels are repainted, renamed and issued with new documents to induce shippers to entrust them with new cargoes, which are then stolen in turn.[112] It was first observed in Southeast Asia in the 1970s, and its origins lie in the hull and cargo insurance frauds perpetrated in the region at that time.[113] The number of phantom ship incidents grew progressively each decade from the 1980s onwards, before stopping abruptly in the early years of this century,[114] apart from one failed attempt in 2005. The insurance industry had mounted an inquiry into the hull and cargo insurance frauds in the 1970s, under the banner of the Far East Regional Investigation Team, reporting in the autumn of 1979 and introducing measures that succeeded in reducing the problem, but the gangs responsible, although known to the inquiry, were never brought to trial, perhaps because of the circumstantial nature of the evidence. In most cases, these were the same gangs that went on to perpetrate the more sophisticated phantom ship hijacks that took place from the mid 1980s to 2002.

Ships targeted for phantom ship frauds, for instance the *Global Mars* and the *Doo Yang Jade*,[115] which went through nine name changes during its two-and-half-year career, carried cargo that could be disposed of easily on the black market, such as diesel fuel, kerosene, refined palm oil, rubber and metals. Most of these thefts were believed to be 'to order', prearranged on behalf of buyers, but this was not always the case, and when the ship involved was carrying a mixed cargo, there would be goods that the gangs could not dispose of immediately. In these cases, the cargo would be offloaded, usually onto barges in international waters, and then stored in warehouses in remote locations on land, such as the Zamboanga peninsula in the Philippines.[116]

Away from Somalia, K&R was prevalent at either end of the Malacca Straits between 2003 and 2005, has occurred repeatedly in the southern

Philippines, usually involving local fishermen, and is now becoming increasingly common in Nigeria as the political situation there is leading to greater lawlessness.[117] A total of 31 incidents involving kidnapping were reported between 2000 and 2005 in the Malacca Strait, although it must be assumed that many others were never notified out of concern for the captives' safety, as seafarers have reportedly been killed when ransom demands have not been met.[118] The ships that suffered such attacks in the Malacca Strait were usually fishing boats and small tankers or cargo vessels, none of which had large crews or could be defended effectively.[119] Most targets were local craft. Incidents appeared to decline once the practice gained international attention in 2005, when three crew members of the Japanese tug Idaten were kidnapped by an organised criminal gang. Victims of kidnappings in Southeast Asia were not kept captive on their own ships for months as they have been in Somalia. In Southeast Asia, more effective law enforcement meant that victims had to be moved regularly to avoid police detection.

K&R attacks at the northern end of the Malacca Strait have often been assumed to be the work of Gerakan Aceh Merdeka (GAM), the Acehnese separatist movement.[120] However, it is widely believed in the region that common pirates, and in some cases members of the Indonesian armed forces, were behind at least some of the attacks and that the Acehnese insurgency, while contributing to the phenomenon, also deflected the attention of the authorities away from non-political criminal activities like piracy and kidnapping, much as common criminal activity can act as a distraction from terrorist activity.

Use of Violence
Common and organised pirates are both violent and prepared to kill their victims to avoid detection, though there is some evidence that violence is slightly more favoured by organised gangs. The PRC observed in 2000 that most attacks 'can now be expected to involve casualties of one sort or another'.[121]

Environmental risk
Because common piracy is unguided and uncoordinated and therefore more accident prone than organised piracy, it potentially presents a greater threat of disruption to economically vital waterways, and of environmental damage to the fisheries and fragile ecosystems that adjoin shipping channels in some regions. Crews may be distracted or possibly imprisoned in their quarters during an attack, such that control of the ship is lost for a

time, risking collision or grounding that could result in significant marine pollution.

The governments of Malaysia and Singapore and some academic observers have rated the dangers posed by such an environmental disaster as potentially more serious than any others posed by piracy.[122] The consequences for a local economy of the loss of valuable fishing grounds or the use of waterways during a clean-up operation would be severe, with possible knock-on security effects.

Access to markets

Pirates need trustworthy intermediaries to dispose of stolen goods and convert foreign currency. In those parts of Indonesia such as the coastal villages of Sumatra where common pirates might be regarded as benefactors of the poor, they are probably able to sell marine equipment and crews' valuables directly to local buyers. But the gangs that steal whole cargoes, or ships, or ships and cargoes together, need larger markets, which are often abroad. In many cases of organised piracy the speed of an operation would seem to indicate that pirates know where to dispose of goods before they steal them; some probably steal to order. These larger-scale operations respond to market demand, and continue, or resume, whenever buyers can obtain what they want from pirates more cheaply than they can from a legitimate supplier. Risk is the deciding factor: governments and law enforcement agencies aiming to cut trade in stolen goods may, through police activity and political pressure, be able to increase the risk to buyers of engaging in such trading practices more successfully than they can increase risk to the pirate suppliers. Nonetheless, illegal markets are not the same as legal markets. As Pino Arlacchi, a senior official of the UN Office for Drug Control and Crime Prevention, has written: '… some of the dynamics of criminal markets are substantially different from those that drive legal markets. Illegal enterprises can resort to the use of violence and intimidation [and can] also corrupt those who should uphold the law and those who are in a position to manipulate public institutions'.[123]

China was the world's biggest market for smuggled goods during the 1990s,[124] and there were active connections between Chinese interests and Indonesian piracy. As Chalk wrote at the time: 'there is a widespread belief that major criminal syndicates retain close links with, or have access to, corrupt government officials, particularly in southern China'.[125] Since the turn of the century, the Chinese government appears to have taken steps to crack down on pirate activity in order to be regarded as a legitimate trading nation, but in practice its ports and markets remain open to stolen goods.[126] The relationship between the state and commerce is close in China, sometimes so much so that, as the IMB Deputy Director Jayant Abhyankar observed, illicit goods are protected by agents of the state: the cargo stolen from the MV *Harpers* in 1993 was, for example, stored under armed guard at an army camp in Guangxi Province.[127]

If one market for stolen cargo closes or contracts, others open: it appears that goods acquired through piracy have been making their way to India and Iran in recent years.[128] Smaller markets also exist in parts of Indonesia, the Philippines and Vietnam, and in Nigeria and Bangladesh.

Links to insurgent or terrorist groups
Despite perpetual speculation about connections between pirates and terrorists, there is no clear evidence of any links. This lack of evidence has not put an end to 'uncritically repeated myths, half truths, and unsupportable assertions of an alleged nexus of piracy and terrorism'.[129] Nevertheless, while it would seem that theories that pirates might use their expertise to teach terrorists how to undermine trade, or for that matter hijack vessels, are baseless, changes to the financing of many terrorist groups over the past couple of decades have brought about some convergence between insurgent and terrorist groups and organised crime networks, creating a potential *indirect* link between terrorism and organised piracy. Also, the presence of pirate activity in a locality can confuse intelligence efforts aimed at tracing terrorists, and distract investigators from their proper targets. The fact that some insurgent groups that engage in terrorism – particularly those in South and Southeast Asia (notably the Liberation Tigers of Tamil Eelam (LTTE), GAM and the Philippine Islamist Abu Sayyaf Group (ASG)) – have also used piratical methods to raise money contributes to this problem.

Levels of official support and corruption
Common piracy flourishes in weak and 'failed' states. It can only be suppressed by on-shore police work and contained by vigorous maritime patrolling. Weak states can often afford neither. Where they can, the forces nominally responsible for suppressing or containing piracy can be in league with the pirates or, in some cases, actually *are* the pirates, which appears to have been the case on occasion in Indonesia. Various factors can bring about such corruption, such as piracy's cultural acceptability, low or non-existent pay and inadequate supervision, or clan or ethnic differences between local authorities and central government, which prompt local officials to support members of their own community against the centre.

Organised criminal pirates can enjoy the support from those in power. Because frauds like phantom ship scams are big business, they bring organised criminals together with corrupt officials and politicians. The suspicion among analysts of maritime crime is that organised pirates in most pirate-prone areas have benefited from the protection of the more senior provincial officials, police officers, and even national politicians, though evidence is naturally scarce because of the sensitivity of the subject.

Even in cases of the most basic common piracy, people other than the pirates will know about their activities, will benefit from them or be forced to tolerate them. The more money a gang makes, the more sophisticated it needs to be in order to manage and protect itself, and thus the more people come under its influence, often willingly. As the historian Peter Earle has written: 'Piracy has always benefited from the support of unscrupulous great men, only to happy to receive bribes and cheap pirated goods at no risk to themselves'.[130]

The Corruption Perceptions Index calculated annually by the Internet Center for Corruption Research scores countries between 0 (highly corrupt) and 10 (very clean) according to the perceptions of business people and analysts across the world. All the countries highlighted here as having a piracy problem or providing a market for goods stolen by pirates scored low on the 2006 index: China 3.3, Philippines 2.5, Indonesia 2.4, Nigeria 2.2, Bangladesh 2.0 (Somalia no data, but 2.1 in 2005). By comparison, two countries that suffer the effects of piracy, but are taking concerted action against it, score more highly: Malaysia 5.5 and Singapore 9.4.[131]

Links to organised crime

Corruption becomes more important to the piracy process the more connections a gang has to criminal networks: corruption and organised crime are rarely separable. In light of the extensive backing enjoyed by the most organised of the pirate gangs from criminal networks on land, the longer states persist in seeing piracy as a sea-based problem, rather than a land-based one with a maritime dimension, the longer it will flourish.

While weak or 'failed' states can provide pirates with useful sanctuary and safe harbours, they are unlikely to be the headquarters of the 'organising minds', the gangsters who lead the operations, about whom very little is known for certain. They are based in more congenial cities. The nearest law-enforcement bodies have come to these figures is arresting their intermediaries, men such as 'Captain Changco', who operated out of a hotel overlooking Manila Bay where he reputedly charged $350,000 to hijack a ship and dispose of the crew before his arrest in 1992, and Chew

Cheng Kiat, or 'Mr Wong', an Indonesian-based Singaporean national who organised some of the most notorious pirate attacks in the Malacca Strait, including the *Petro Ranger* and *Atalanta* hijacks, before he was arrested in 1999.[132]

Even if the pirates themselves are caught and a trail of evidence leads back to the organising minds, the complexity of the international extradition procedure, and the difficulties of following a trail of evidence from an attack in international waters to its organisational origins in a different state from the pirates' own, allied to the lack of will on the part of many states to pursue such cases, means that those who direct major piracy operations are effectively immune from prosecution. In addition, some of them have political influence, and can count on tacit support from the authorities.[133]

Contemporary piracy: local second-order problem, or threat to international security?

Piracy is a potential threat to all seafarers in the areas where it occurs. Those most at risk are users of smaller craft such as fishing boats, tugs and smaller cargo ships. Large ships passing through piracy-prone areas run a low risk of being attacked, especially if they take precautions. The communities that are affected most directly by piracy are villages and small ports in pirate areas, where often both the victims and collusive officials will live.

The international community has only been affected indirectly so far by piracy and this is unlikely to change. Common piracy is a menace to its victims and an irritation to littoral states and shipping companies, but is not usually a wider concern. However, as Figure 3 indicates, there are theoretically a number of ways in which pirate activity could pose a threat to international security. Waterways crucial to international trade, particularly those that are vulnerable to interruption, for instance through a hijacked ship blocking a narrow strait, could become a source of insecurity beyond the locality if trade were severely adversely affected, particularly if no other routes were available. Vessels carrying oil and gas could, if hijacked by pirates, pose a danger to security because of their cargoes; likewise those carrying nuclear materials. Most naval and military equipment and personnel is usually transported on civilian vessels, which if hijacked would also have potentially serious security consequences.

But while such potential (and, in the case of the latter two, remote) scenarios are worth acknowledging, they are of marginal concern: the great majority of pirate attacks have only local effects. However, the state

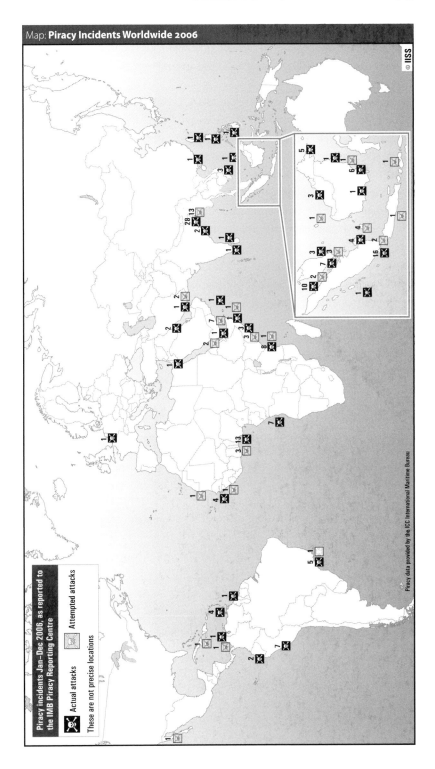

Map: **Piracy Incidents Worldwide 2006**

weakness and cultural acceptance of piracy that coexist in a number of affected states create a favourable environment for the most serious form of the problem, highly organised piracy, to function in a way that can be said to pose a wider threat.

Organised crime can destabilise weak states through the corruption it fuels, as has been the case in El Salvador and Guatemala beginning in the early 1990s, and it can unsettle stronger ones, as now appears to be happening in Mexico.[134] Where piracy is an element of organised crime in a given state, as Peter Chalk observes: '[It] can play a ... role in undermining and weakening political stability by encouraging corruption among elected government officials'.[135]

The most sophisticated pirate attacks demand a wide network of contacts to provide documents and political protection, and dispose of goods. Without some degree of official connivance in countries where goods stolen by pirates are sold, organised pirate gangs would struggle to continue operating at such a level. As long, however, as this connivance persists, and the suppression of piracy remains a low political priority for governments of affected states, such as Indonesia and Nigeria, and as long as organised crime and political corruption coexist and thus continue to hamper effective law enforcement on land while pirates exploit the limitations of the law as it relates to both high and territorial seas, the problem of organised piracy will remain and its effects will continue. These effects will, furthermore, extend via wider crime networks beyond the area or state where attacks take place to other states, where the proceeds can be used to fund other crimes and weaken other polities through corruption. This process can have consequences for regional and potentially international security.

CHAPTER TWO

Maritime Terrorism

The number of terrorist attacks at sea has been minuscule as a proportion of terrorist attacks overall.[1] According to the RAND Corporation's Terrorism Chronology Database and the RAND–MIPT Terrorism Incident Database, incidents of maritime terrorism account for only 2% of all the terrorism incidents recorded over the past 30 years.[2] This is because the conditions necessary for a successful terrorist attack can be fulfilled on water only with difficulty. Terrorists have not operated at sea to any great extent so far because they can operate more easily and effectively on land. For the majority of terrorist groups operating today, maritime activity is unnecessary; there are only a few groups for whom maritime operations are driven by a strategic or operational imperative.

Terrorism at sea: major events

The incident that for many people still epitomises terrorism at sea is the hijack of a cruise ship, the *Achille Lauro,* in the Mediterranean in 1985. Terrorists from the Abu Abbas faction of the Palestine Liberation Front took over the ship and demanded that Israel release Palestinian prisoners, which Tel Aviv refused to do. One hostage, an American, Leon Klinghoffer, was shot and thrown overboard. The terrorists eventually secured a deal with Egypt, surrendering the ship in return for safe passage to Tunis. The US was not party to this deal, and forced the aircraft carrying the ten hijackers to land in Italy. However, the US was prevented from trying Klinghoffer's killers under its own jurisdiction, and though the hijacking led to the signing of the SUA, this agreement has had very little practical application.[3]

For 15 years after the *Achille Lauro*, there were very few terror events at sea against Western targets. Then, in October 2000, al-Qaeda operatives attacked and nearly succeeded in sinking the *Arleigh Burke*-class destroyer USS *Cole* in Aden harbour. Seventeen sailors died and 39 were injured. Caught by surprise, one of the most advanced warships afloat, designed to protect carrier battle groups, was unable to defend itself against two men in a rubber dinghy packed with explosives.[4] Two years later the oil tanker MV *Limburg* was struck in a similar way by a small, fast-moving craft in another al-Qaeda attack.

The deadliest maritime terrorist attack to date was mounted against a passenger vessel. In February 2004 the 10,000-tonne *SuperFerry 14* suffered an explosion and subsequent fire as it left Manila harbour. The explosion killed 63 people immediately; of the 717 people who jumped overboard, 53 died or were missing, presumed dead. The ASG claimed responsibility.[5]

Factors that contribute to the success of maritime terrorism

Groups that practise terrorism use the sea to a varying extent. Those that have exploited the sea most effectively have, in the main, done so out of operational necessity: because they have needed to land forces on an exposed flank, for instance, or in order to protect supply lines. The need for supplies from abroad meant that the LTTE was compelled to build a maritime capability, as was GAM in Aceh, for the same reason. Groups that have lacked these kinds of practical imperatives have generally abandoned their maritime activities.

Necessity is the maritime terrorists' equivalent of pirates' opportunity: a primary motivator. As with opportunity, it is never the only one, and it is not enough to ensure success. Six major factors contribute to the effective operation of a terrorist group at sea:

- Legal and jurisdictional weakness
- Geographical necessity
- Inadequate security
- Secure base areas
- Maritime tradition
- Charismatic and effective leadership
- State support

There is considerable overlap with the factors that facilitate piracy. Like them, these factors interact with each other and, while circumstances determine which predominates, all are usually present in some degree wherever groups that use terrorism are active at sea.

Legal and jurisdiction weakness

Some states see political advantage in giving cover to terrorists and insurgents through bases, either on land, or in their territorial waters, as in the case of Tunisia, Libya and Yemen in relation to the Palestine Liberation Organisation (PLO). The waters of weak states that lack the means or motivation to pursue illegal actors may also provide a haven. Furthermore, as law enforcement officials have only limited rights to board the vessels of other flag states on the high seas and in their exclusive economic zones (EEZs) (the portion of the sea, up to 200nm from the coast, over which a state has special rights over marine resources), terrorists may use the vessels of complicit states and even containers to hide their activities. This legal limitation has almost certainly also played a role in nuclear proliferation.

Geography

In most but not all cases, necessity is determined by geography. The geography of the region where they operated meant that the Nicaraguan Contras did not *need* to use the sea, nor does al-Qaeda; consequently, these groups' investment in a maritime capability is not as great as that of groups operating in regions where the sea is strategically crucial. Sri Lanka, for instance, is a divided island, meaning that the Sri Lankan Navy (SLN) could place severe limitations on the Tamil rebellion simply by imposing a blockade. Faced with this vulnerability, the LTTE has invested in a naval capability robust enough to neutralise the SLN, although it has never been sufficiently strong to defeat it. Geographical necessity has enabled in this case the creation of the most successful maritime insurgency currently in operation. Similarly, Israel's tightly controlled land borders meant that insurgents such as the PLO successfully developed maritime capabilities in order to be able to mount coastal raids from bases in Lebanon.

Inadequate security

In the maritime domain, the effect that state security activity can have on the success of insurgencies using terror is most clearly demonstrated by the contrast between what the two most determined and resourceful maritime insurgencies have been able to achieve. The Sea Tigers ('Kadal Puli' in Tamil), the maritime arm of the LTTE, have fought the SLN to a virtual stalemate. In contrast, although Palestinian insurgent groups, Fatah in particular, were largely successful at sea until 1982 and continued to have some success until 1985, especially in landing raiding parties, the elimination of their Lebanese base areas and renewed security efforts on the part of the Israel Defense Forces (IDF) Navy since then have meant that Israeli forces now enjoy, and have enjoyed for some time, almost complete control of the maritime area bordering Israel and Lebanon. The navy has reduced coastal raiding to negligible levels and imposed severe (although by no means total) restrictions on Palestinian logistical activity at sea.

In Southeast Asia, GAM, the ASG, the separatist Moro Islamic Liberation Front (MILF), Jemaah Islamiah and other insurgent groups that need to transport personnel and supplies by sea have benefited from under-investment in maritime security on the part of Indonesia and the Philippines, and generally weak security cooperation among the states in the region, although there are signs that the situation is beginning to improve.

Secure base areas

All insurgent groups need secure base areas for planning, rest, logistical support and training, but the fact that people cannot live permanently at sea and depend on the reliable operation of boats to travel on it make those operating at sea arguably more dependent on bases than their land-based counterparts. In the 1970s and early 1980s, Palestinian insurgent groups ran maritime operations out of a string of small workshops and bases along the Lebanese coast, with a particular concentration around Tripoli in the north. When Israel invaded Lebanon in 1982 and dispersed the PLO, Libya became the nearest maritime base area; others were even further away in Tunisia and Algeria. This seriously restricted the Palestinians' maritime options, and less effective maritime activity resulted.

However, an organisation's determination affects how it copes with the destruction of its bases. The disatrous effect of the 2004 tsunami on GAM, for instance, prompted the organisation to close down its entire operation. By contrast, the LTTE's Sea Tigers, which lost more than 2,000 personnel plus boats and other equipment (including four coastal radars) to the tsunami, quickly replaced the lost equipment and resumed operations.[6]

Maritime tradition

To operate beyond the sheltered waters of a port or harbour, a terrorist group needs either to have maritime training or to be in a position to draw on the support and skills of a maritime community. Palestinian insurgent groups have learnt from and cooperated with smugglers ever since they began maritime operations in the late 1960s. More recently, they have hidden smuggling boats amongst the Gaza fishing fleet, which would not be possible without the fishermen's collaboration.

Two groups in particular, the ASG and the Sea Tigers, enjoy close connections with a seafaring tradition. The ASG's personnel are mostly Tausug, a Muslim ethnic group indigenous to the Sulu archipelago in the Philippines. According to Philippine terrorism expert Rommel Banlaoi, the ASG draws its members from 'families with strong, centuries-old seafaring traditions. Their deep knowledge of the maritime domain gives them ample capability to conduct maritime terrorism.'[7] Historically, the pirates of the archipelago were notorious for raiding coastal towns and villages in search of slaves: the ASG's reputation for coastal raiding and hostage-taking can be viewed in terms of this tradition.

The LTTE's maritime capability is equally well rooted in local seafaring communities, particularly in the town of Valvettiturai on the Jaffna peninsula, which has a long-standing reputation as a smuggling centre.[8] The Indian writer V. Suryanarayan describes 'a close nexus among fishermen, smugglers and Tamil militants' and observes that the group's founder, Velupillai Prabhakaran, and other LTTE leaders grew up in the town.[9] Vijay Sakhuja writes of a 'cohesive community held together by ties of kinship and caste. There were links between its smugglers, fisher folk and ordinary tradesmen.'[10]

It is in such contexts that a long-standing relationship between piracy and maritime terrorism can be seen. It is in Southeast Asia primarily, but also in Sri Lanka, that groups that use terror for political ends – the MILF, the Moro National Liberation Front (MNLF), the ASG, GAM and the LTTE – also display piratical behaviour; taking hostages, extorting money and stealing from ships.

Charismatic and effective leadership

Visionary leadership exercised with determination can overcome many obstacles. Al-Qaeda emerged from the deserts and mountains of Saudi Arabia and Afghanistan. It had no pressing need to mount attacks at sea, lacked maritime experience and had no obvious maritime tradition upon which to draw. Yet it launched two of the most effective maritime terrorist attacks in history and planned several more. This success can partly be ascribed to the organisational ability and personal charisma of its principal maritime strategist, Abd al-Rahim al-Nashiri, who was probably able to draw on the experience of Yemeni fishermen and boatbuilders for the practical expertise he needed.[11] The momentum went out of al-Qaeda's maritime operations when al-Nashiri was captured in 2002. This was not due solely to his loss: al-Nashiri's arrest was part of an international campaign that captured and killed other leaders, destroyed base areas and placed serious restrictions on al-Qaeda's operational freedom.[12] Nevertheless, his absence is a major factor in the contraction of al-Qaeda's maritime activities, and finding a replacement with comparable ability will not be easy.

State support

State support, via the provision of arms or bases or both, can compensate for weakness or gaps in a group's capability and can enable a group to mount larger operations than it would be able to undertake alone. The Nicaraguan Contras, for example, might or might not have operated effectively without US assistance, but the likelihood is that without it they would have been unable to launch their major maritime operations, such as the mining of Nicaragua's major ports.[13]

Palestinian insurgents have over the years received substantial assistance from diverse sources, including the Soviet Union, Czechoslovakia, Yugoslavia and Arab states. Although the PLO in particular has had talented maritime commanders, the extent to which these groups' maritime operations would have been successful without this extensive and continuing external support is doubtful. As it is, Palestinian naval operations pushed Israel hard until Israel's 1982 invasion of Lebanon and the closure of the Palestinian coastal bases there.

External state support to Palestinian insurgent organisations continues. In the case of Hizbullah, it now possibly includes the provision by Iran of sophisticated anti-ship missiles and the technicians needed to maintain and fire them.

Weapons and tools

While ships can in theory be attacked anywhere they can float, most terrorists do not possess the capabilities of even coastal navies and are, therefore, unlikely to mount attacks on ships a long way from the shore. Within this limitation, however, there are a number of ways in which attacks may be launched.

Small boats

A rigid-hulled inflatable boat or a small recreational craft will usually be capable of delivering the equivalent of a car bomb, and small craft such as these equipped with waterborne improvised explosive devices (IEDs) present the most serious contemporary maritime terrorist threat.

With the exception of the *Achille Lauro* attack and the attacks mounted on Philippine inter-island ferries using planted bombs, every significant maritime terrorist strike so far has been carried out using small boats. The USS *Cole* and the MV *Limburg* were both struck by small boats equipped with waterborne IEDs. Though Khalid Sheikh Mohammed, the architect of the 11 September attacks, and Abd al-Rahim al-Nashiri both considered using large ships for attacks, and might have done so had they not been captured,[14] they, like most other terrorists, favoured the use of small boats. One reason for this may be caution: terrorists tend to operate with comparatively few resources at their disposal, so adaptation and incremental adjustment of methods are preferred to revolutionary changes in tactics: if a radical new operation fails, money and materials are wasted.[15]

Small boats have various practical advantages: they are often fast, or if not fast can accelerate rapidly, which can be more important. They are highly manoeuvrable. They can be difficult to detect because they sit low in the water, and often possess a small or non-existent radar signature. They are inexpensive enough to be used in multiples, so that attacks can be mounted from different directions, and anonymous enough to be hidden amongst other small craft such as fishing vessels and pleasure boats.[16] They are also appropriate for the less spectacular, less ambitious and more opportunistic attacks that currently appear to be preferred across the terrorist spectrum.[17] Nevertheless, they can also be employed for more ambitious attacks: in theory small boats could not only damage a target vessel, but also cause wider disruption, if they were used to ram a large ship, either when it was entering a harbour, thus blocking the harbour's entrance, or when it was discharging a volatile cargo at a terminal.

They have their limitations for offensive operations, however. Hitting a ship accurately, even a stationary one, is notoriously difficult. Furthermore, the attack on the *Limburg*, in which one small craft was driven into the side of the target, causing serious but not irreparable damage, appeared to show that in order for enough ordnance to be delivered to inflict long-term harm, the coordinated action of several fast-moving boats is needed. This requires detailed planning; and preparing such boats covertly, placing them in the water undetected, manoeuvring them in restricted harbour waters or operating them at sea in other than calm conditions are all high-risk activities. The *Limburg* attack also demonstrated that an explosive charge detonated against an outer hull would have difficulty breaching an inner hull, meaning that the damage caused would not necessarily disable the ship. The suggestion has been made that maritime terrorists could solve this problem by mimicking the recent development in land attacks whereby one car or truck bomb is used to breach the target's defences and is followed by a second which drives through the debris and is detonated closer to the target, causing the maximum damage.[18] Replicating this tactic at sea, particularly if the target was still moving or able to defend itself, would be extremely difficult. An immediate follow-on attack would run into turbulence and backwash, and a vessel attempting a delayed attack might have to take aim at a breach that is already partially submerged or obscured by smoke and flame.

Naval mines

The more inconspicuous and highly effective possible supplement or alternative to the IED is the naval mine.[19] In addition to new designs, older and cheaper mines can be made more effective with electronic upgrades that can enable them to select particular vessel profiles. One advantage of mines from a terrorist's point of view is that they are time-consuming and expensive to remove. They can be planted quickly and covertly in large numbers and can cause major damage, potentially imposing substantial costs on the target state if laid in a busy harbour. In 1984, for example, just 39 mines laid by Contra groups in three Nicaraguan ports had a significant effect on the national economy. Terrorists using mines only need to explode one major target, or simply re-lay the mines on an irregular basis, to achieve their aim of inducing fear and insecurity. Nevertheless, despite their advantages, mines do not appear to have attracted widespread interest from terrorist groups, though al-Nashiri did consider the use of limpet mines. In recent years, only the LTTE has actually used mines, including remote-controlled versions, which were first deployed off the Jaffna peninsula in the early 1990s.

Divers and 'human torpedoes'

Terrorist use of divers first came to public attention in 2002, when an al-Qaeda operative reportedly revealed a plan to attack US navy ships with bomb-laden divers while they visited an Indonesian port. In 2005, ASG operative Gamal Baharan revealed that he had been sent to a training camp in Palawan in the Philippines to prepare for an underwater suicide-bomb attack that was being planned by Jemaah Islamiah groups closely connected to al-Qaeda.[20] But reports like these are rare and often unreliable, and, while clearly some activity in these areas has taken place, most analysts are sceptical about its extent.

The LTTE Sea Tigers were among the first non-state actors to use divers offensively. Their efforts were initially hampered by their use of normal open-circuit diving equipment, which meant that a number of swimmers were killed in 1986 when air bubbles rising to the surface of the water gave them away. After this incident, the Tigers invested in 're-breather' kits that enabled swimmers to breathe using recirculated air, and they continue to use divers in their operations: in 2006, Sea Tiger swimmers, who had apparently been intending to fix mines to the hulls of naval patrol boats, were arrested when they came ashore close to Colombo.[21] The Tigers have also succeeded in developing a semi-submersible 'human torpedo' or 'suicide scooter', guided to its target by a single operative equipped with diving gear, which has been used in at least two successful attacks.[22] Both al-Qaeda and the Sea Tigers have shown an interest in acquiring swimmer delivery vehicles, small submersible craft for transporting swimmers closer to their target.[23]

Submarines

A submarine presents a greater threat to shipping than does a diver, as it enables skilled operators to mount an attack over a longer range, with more accuracy and with a heavier payload than could be accomplished by a bomb-laden swimmer, even one assisted by a swimmer delivery vehicle. But it is highly unlikely that any terrorist group, unless heavily state sponsored, would possess the capability and resources to purchase and operate a properly equipped attack submarine offensively. An organisation would need trained, experienced personnel who had served in a submarine-equipped navy in order to be able to use fully submersible craft for attack operations.

Operating and building simple submarines for smuggling missions, however, is an option for a number of terrorist groups. Well-resourced criminal gangs have also built submarines, usually for drug-smuggling operations, confirming that it is well within the capabilities of non-state actors.[24] Two small submarines intended for drug smuggling were seized off the Colombian port of Santa Marta in 1997;[25] in 2000 a cocaine cartel in Colombia was close to completing a large submarine near Bogota; in 2005 another small submarine was discovered half-finished in Tumaco, Colombia; and in 2006 a mini-submarine loaded with cocaine was seized off Costa Rica by a multinational task force.[26]

The Sea Tigers have long sought a full submersion capability, and, along with some anti-Israel insurgents, have pioneered the use of submarines by non-state actors. In 1999 there was a report that the MILF in the southern Philippines had made enquiries about buying a mini-submarine from North Korea,[27] but the majority of accounts of this kind of activity relate to the LTTE. Most famously, the Tigers' attempts to build a submarine in Phuket, Thailand were exposed in 2000,[28] along with three more mini-submarines under construction in a village south of the town.[29] Reports have circulated in recent years that the Tigers planned to buy mini-submarines from North Korea and a submarine from South Africa, but no evidence has emerged to indicate that these purchases were made.[30] In March 2007, there was a report from India that the LTTE could once again be trying to build a mini-submarine.[31]

Missiles

On 14 July 2006, an Israeli naval corvette, the *Hanit*, was badly damaged while patrolling off the coast of Lebanon by what was believed to be an Iranian-built subsonic C-802 anti-ship missile fired from an area under the control of Hizbullah.[32] A second ship sailing nearby was hit by an identical missile at approximately the same time.[33] The consensus until recently has been that only states are capable of buying, maintaining and operating such sophisticated weapons and that they would not allow them to be used by their proxies. While this still broadly holds, the evidence in this case is equivocal. If Iranian forces were not in Lebanon when the attack took place, then these firings represent a substantial increase, either in terrorist firepower, or in the level of state support enjoyed by Hizbullah. The IDF's view is that now, with the exception of the long-range *Shihab* missile, 'Hizbullah has everything Iran has'.[34]

Other weaponry

Weapons that are available, relatively cheap and simple to operate – though basic in comparison to C-802s, and with varying degrees of usefulness for maritime terrorists – include:

- Anti-tank guided weapons: not ideal for attacking maritime targets because of their short range, they have not yet been used at sea. Moreover their warheads, which are designed to penetrate heavy armour, would be apt to pass straight through the hulls of most ships without causing an explosion
- Rocket-propelled grenades (RPGs): their range is limited, but, as pirates have demonstrated, they can halt a vessel if fired at the engine spaces or the accommodation block
- Heavy machine guns: these could achieve a result similar to that of RPGs if fired at the same areas

- Mortars: against a moving target mortars would be largely ineffective. They could, however, inflict damage on ships tied up in port. The left-wing Portuguese terrorist group FP-25 claimed responsibility for an (unsuccessful) attack in 1985 when a 60mm mortar was used to attack NATO warships in Lisbon harbour[35]
- *Katyusha*-style rockets: these are of limited use because they are inaccurate. However they were used (unsuccessfully) against US navy ships visiting Aqaba in 2005[36]
- Man-portable Air Defence Systems (MANPADS): these shoulder-launched anti-aircraft weapons are widely available. MANPADS that home in on infrared emissions would be able to pick up heat from the stacks of target ships, but they are not likely to be powerful enough to cause major damage

All of these weapons are most likely to hit their target if fired from the shore at ships that are either stationary in port, or moving very slowly through a narrow channel. They could be mounted on small craft but in most cases the chances of achieving a successful hit are low in the absence of a stabilised mounting.

Methods and targets

Though the current terrorist preference appears to be for much smaller-scale operations, it is nevertheless helpful to use the 2001 assaults on New York and Washington to identify major elements in a successful terrorist attack, and then transfer those elements to the maritime domain in order to see how they might be replicated at sea.

The 11 September attackers exploited the inherent features of aircraft to turn them into guided weapons without any form of modification. The targets of the attacks were iconic symbols of American power. The Twin Towers were also an economic target; their destruction imposed a serious cost on the American economy. They were also, of course, a mass casualty target.

With these elements in mind, the possibilities for terrorism at sea can be broken down into four broad categories:

- Ships as iconic targets
- Ships/offshore installations as economic targets
- Ships as mass-casualty targets
- Ships/other vehicles as weapons

Some of the possibilities in these categories have already been realised by terrorists, others remain only potential threats.

Ships as iconic targets

Few cargo ships nowadays are so closely linked to a state that an attack on one would be seen as an attack on the flag state. Warships and a limited number of cruise ships (for example the *Queen Mary 2*), however, are iconic representatives of their state, and as such are attractive targets for terrorists. In addition to the USS *Cole*, attacks have been attempted by al-Qaeda on the USS *The Sullivans*, in January 2000, also in Aden, and on the USS *Ashland* and USS *Kearsarge* while they were visiting the Jordanian port of Aqaba in 2005; an al-Qaeda plan to attack a US warship in Singapore was uncovered in 2001; and a plot, probably conceived by al-Nashiri, to attack a US warship in the Strait of Hormuz was planned for the same year.[37] A plan to attack US and British warships in the Strait of Gibraltar, again by al-Qaeda, was foiled the following year. It is possible that other planned and attempted attacks on warships have also been disrupted.

Ships/offshore installations as economic targets

In a tape released in 2004, Bin Laden stated that al-Qaeda had a 'policy [of] bleeding America to the point of bankruptcy'.[38] Oil is the obvious focus for such a policy, and tankers are a vital component of the US oil industry's critical infrastructure. Two years after the attack on the *Cole*, in October 2002, the oil tanker MV *Limburg* (now the *Maritime Jewel*) was struck, again off Yemen, by al-Qaeda operatives. But the economic consequences of the attack fell mainly on Yemen. Insurance rates for ships calling at Yemeni ports increased immediately and substantially, and shippers of all types of goods stayed away for a time.[39] The wider economic consequences of the *Limburg* attack were limited. Oil prices increased by 1.3% within hours, but fell back quickly, though admittedly in a period of slack demand. In a tight oil market, troubled by the effects of political turbulence, particularly in the Middle East, the effects could have been more serious.

Prior to his capture, al-Nashiri was reportedly planning to attack several oil tankers as they passed through the Strait of Hormuz. Presumably the hope was that if several ships could be sunk close together, they would block the strait for a sufficient period of time to disrupt the oil market. One tanker sinking, probably even several, however, would be unlikely to cause major economic repercussions. Certainly, to inflict economic hardship sufficiently severe to affect US government policy, a terrorist group would need to reduce the world's – or at least the United States' – oil supply significantly, for instance by destroying a major refinery.[40]

It makes more sense for terrorist groups to attack production facilities, oil and gas terminals and refineries than to target tankers. Al-Qaeda has carried out attacks on oil installations in Saudi Arabia, and multiple attacks have been mounted against oil installations in Iraq, seriously degrading its oil production, impeding the reconstruction process and damaging the economy. However a maritime component to these assaults has been limited. In a rare incident, in April 2004, a dhow and two smaller boats approached Iraqi oil terminals six miles off Basra. As an interception boat sent to investigate pulled alongside it, the dhow exploded, killing three US sailors. The two smaller craft then moved towards the terminals at high speed but exploded before they made contact.[41] Abu Musab al-Zarqawi, then leader of al-Qaeda in Mesopotamia, claimed responsibility. Oil prices rose, but fell again quickly as they had after the *Limburg* attack.

Similar attempts have not been made since,[42] but the sensitivity of the international commerce system to interruptions in the movement of goods and fluctuations in commodity prices means that successful attacks on economic targets could in the right circumstances have serious consequences for the world economy.

Ships as mass-casualty targets

There has been little public discussion of maritime terrorism aimed at causing large-scale casualties, but ever since the *Achille Lauro* hijack, terrorist-watchers have been awaiting another attack on a cruise ship.[43] So far none has occurred, although plans for an attack on an Israeli cruise ship in Turkey in 2005 were well advanced before they were disrupted.[44] Cruise ships are well built with many internal structural sub-divisions, and are consequently hard to sink, but the heat and smoke generated by a *Limburg*-style assault could well result in the death and injury of large numbers of passengers in the resulting panic.

Cruise ships also offer an opportunity for mass hostage-taking. This type of attack would almost certainly be mounted after internal seizure by terrorists posing as passengers or infiltrated as crew, or a combination of both, and would therefore probably be more difficult to achieve than an external attack, given the airport-type screening through which passengers and crew must pass[45] – in the years since the *Achille Lauro*, cruise-ship security has been stepped up considerably.[46] Hijacking a large ship is in any case a much more challenging operation than taking over an aircraft, because of the number of passengers and crew a necessarily small number of terrorists would need to subdue and then control. This might not, however, be a problem in every case. Depending on the configuration of the ship, it might be possible for terrorists to gain control by taking over the bridge and a relatively small number of passengers.

Despite greater interest among analysts in the possibility of an attack on a cruise ship, it remains the case that open-access ferries, such as the *SuperFerry* 14 bombed in 2004, are probably the most likely targets for mass-casualty attacks, including possible hostage-taking, at sea.

Ships/other vehicles as weapons

Ships: The idea of using a large, or medium-sized, ship as a weapon is a 'scaling-up' of the idea of using civilian airliners as weapons. The reasoning is that if two relatively small objects, airliners, can cause considerable destruction, then ships, which are much larger, could, if laden with suitably volatile cargoes, cause commensurately more damage.[47] Their limitation, of course, is that they could only be detonated with serious effect in ports or a few vital waterways (though al-Qaeda has reportedly considered exploding ships further out to sea in order to destroy other vessels in their vicinity).

Once a hostile vessel were inside a harbour, unprepared defenders would be able to do little to prevent an explosion. Two historical instances demonstrate how devastating the effects could be.[48] On 6 December 1917 in Halifax, Nova Scotia, the French munitions ship *Mont Blanc*, which had been carrying over 2,500 tonnes of benzol fuel, TNT, picric acid and gun cotton, blew up in the harbour. More than 1,600 people were killed immediately. The eventual death toll rose to over 2,000, with up to 9,000 injured, including between 200 and 600 people who lost their sight.[49] In Texas City in 1947 the *Grandcamp*, thought to have been loaded with about 2,300 tonnes of ammonium nitrate, probably intended for use as an agricultural fertiliser,[50] exploded as the result of a fire with a force that shattered windows in Houston 40 miles away, creating a shockwave that was felt 250 miles away in Louisiana. This shockwave set the nearby Monsanto Chemical plant on fire. The fire spread, via pipelines, to other plants in the surrounding area. The *High Flyer* was also in port that day, loaded with sulphur and 1,000 tonnes of ammonium nitrate. It too exploded, but with even greater force. Estimates put the number of dead at more than 600, with 3,500 injured, and property to the value of $67 million ($1 billion at current values) was destroyed.

The quantities of ammonium nitrate being traded between the world's ports are sufficient to tempt any terrorist – Timothy McVeigh needed only two tonnes of it to kill 168 people and injure 800 more when he blew up federal offices in Oklahoma City in 1995, although the mixture he used was probably made more potent by the addition of nitromethane, a fuel used by racing cars.[51] But there are obstacles to achieving an explosion like that of the *Grandcamp*, in addition to the difficulties of hijacking a ship and loading it with such a cargo. In most of its forms ammonium nitrate is stable, and needs to be primed with fuel oil and triggered by an explosive such as Semtex before it can be detonated.[52] If terrorists hijacked an ammonium nitrate carrier its cargo would not be primed. The 11 September model might suggest that the terrorists' first recourse would be prime the ammonium nitrate with the ship's own fuel. But it is difficult to see how the two could be mixed effectively as there is no direct connection between a ship's fuel bunkers and its holds, and rigging such a connection would be almost impossible using the equipment that ships normally carry.

A true parallel with the 11 September attacks would be the exploitation of the destructive potential of a ship's cargo without augmentation, and gas and oil are seen by some as presenting serious risks in this context.

Liquefied natural gas (LNG) and, especially, liquefied petroleum gas (LPG) can be dangerous. But the fuels' weapon potential is open to doubt. Handled properly, LNG is safe. The ships used to transport it are usually amongst the best built, run and maintained in any fleet, so there is little danger while the LNG is on a ship. The danger comes if the liquid vents and mixes with air in a specific ratio. If the liquid were released in a quantity large enough not to vaporise immediately, it could form a pool on the surface of the water, which if ignited would create a 'pool fire', which could give off substantial radiated heat, making it dangerous to approach. A very large pool fire would probably be extremely difficult to extinguish.[53] But how such a fire might behave has only been determined by relatively small-scale experiments, and it has been suggested that the amount of radiated heat a large pool fire would produce might in fact be significantly lower than these experiments indicate.[54] Furthermore, if terrorists managed to breach a ship's tank they would probably do so with a device that was itself an ignition source, such as an explosive-laden boat, which would ignite the escaping gas the moment it passed through the breach,[55] meaning that a pool would not have a chance to form. It is also quite possible that the fire would fail to spread beyond the one tank.[56] Until large-scale tests are undertaken (or, of course, a real large-scale incident takes place), the likely extent of an LNG fire on or near a ship remains unknowable.[57] This uncertainty is why LNG ships are only allowed to enter and remain in ports under strict supervision and close guard, despite the conclusion of a 2004 report by the US Department of Energy-owned Sandia National Laboratories that risks from accidental spills are small, and risks arising from intentional sabotage could be contained.[58] LPG theoretically has a greater potential for use in terrorism than LNG, because it explodes. However, its explosive potential is unreliable, and is usually only carried in small quantities, so its usefulness to terrorists is in fact limited.

There are other ways in which large ships might be used as weapons. An oil tanker might be run aground in order to cause oil pollution serious enough to close ports, or even critical chokepoints such as the Straits of Malacca or Hormuz, and there is evidence to suggest that al-Qaeda has investigated the possibility of using an oil tanker as a weapon.[59] Alternatively, a large ship, or several large ships, could be sunk to prevent movement through a narrow strait or harbour entrance. This could have major economic consequences, and reports circulated in 2005 indicating that terrorists had considered sinking ships in the Suez Canal. Nevertheless, manoeuvring a large ship to the optimum location without exciting suspicion would demand much technical skill, patience and luck (and in many cases would be impossible without the assistance of tugs). Although such an action would certainly cause major disruption, as long as the necessary lifting gear is available wrecks are not usually long-lasting obstacles.

Terrorists might also be able to use large ships as kinetic weapons by driving them into port facilities or, more likely, into other ships in port carrying volatile cargoes, with the aim of triggering the sort of chain reaction that was seen in the Texas City disaster. This would only be feasible in ports without a narrow entrance channel and where the assistance of neither a pilot nor a tug was required.

While any vessel employed as a weapon would probably either be hijacked or rammed by a small boat or boats to create an explosion or fire, one alternative that has been posited is that terrorists could instead buy or charter a ship to use as a weapon. In this scenario, terrorists would put their own crew on board and, provided they could find a discreet location, take time to make careful preparations for attack. However there are three major objections to this. Firstly, terrorist organisations have limited resources and need to be frugal.[60] Any ship bought would need to be in good condition to avoid arousing suspicion. LNG carriers are hugely expensive, and even smaller ships such as LPG and bulk carriers cost between $6m and $30m. Secondly, even if a ship were chartered for less, it would be extremely difficult to find a trained crew willing to participate. If LNG or LPG were being used, the crew would also need specialist knowledge to be able to release the gas effectively. Finally, there is the challenge of carrying off the deception. The master and crew would have to perform all the normal tasks of ship handling without raising suspicions for days, possibly weeks. The 11 September hijackers only had to keep their nerve for an hour or so. The numbers of people involved and the timescale of the operation would make detection by intelligence operatives extremely hard to avoid. For these reasons, this scenario is very unlikely to take place.

Any use of large ships is a major challenge to terrorists, as such vessels are difficult to control, needing a trained crew to operate them effectively, and acquiring a large ship – either through hijack, purchase or charter – is fraught with problems. Small craft are likely to remain maritime terrorists' weapon of choice for some time to come.

Aircraft: As warships improve their force-protection capabilities with passive defences (including long-range acoustic devices and floating barriers, and sophisticated weaponry such as *Mini Typhoon* electro-optic chain guns and small fast-reaction missiles, supplemented by small arms), and as small craft are increasingly prevented from approaching high-value targets such as oil tankers, gas carriers and cruise ships in ports and harbour approaches, terrorists will need to be able to inflict serious damage from a greater distance. The threat posed by terrorist use of aerial or more sophisticated stand-off weapons may increase in the future as a result.

Small private aircraft could conceivably be employed as flying bombs (though, unlike the aircraft used on 11 September, they would need to be packed with explosives) and al-Nashiri is believed to have considered this option. Large buildings may be able to withstand being hit by small aircraft, as they have on the few occasions when this has happened accidentally,[61] but the impact on a ship could potentially be more serious. Such an operation would, however, be enormously challenging. Loading enough explosives onto an aircraft would present problems in the first instance, given the size of the airframe, and a very highly skilled pilot would be required to locate the target and take accurate aim, even if the ship were stationary. Though possible, this scenario is therefore extremely remote.

Other terrorist uses of the sea

Delivery of weapons

The maritime terrorist threat that has attracted the most attention is the possibility of a freight container being used to deliver a nuclear or radiological bomb.[62] However, there are solid grounds to be sceptical about most postulated nuclear terrorism scenarios.[63] It would be very difficult for any terrorist group to steal an already-assembled device in working order, or to obtain and assemble the necessary technology and components to make one, then deliver the device to the target and detonate it successfully. It would be similarly difficult to obtain the components for and assemble a 'dirty bomb'.[64]

Furthermore, it is unlikely that terrorist organisations, which tend to be risk-averse, would attempt to deliver either type of weapon in a container.[65] Given the investment necessary to build or obtain a nuclear or radiological device, it is hard to imagine that a terrorist group would entrust something so valuable to the vagaries of the international transport system. Sophisticated weapons are usually sensitive to temperature, humidity and movement. In many cases their mission-readiness declines if they are not carefully maintained.[66] Containers are frequently misplaced, stolen, delayed, dropped, broken open, left out in the sun, drenched with seawater, lost overboard and set on fire. Terrorists probably do smuggle equipment, components, money and even personnel in containers, but they are unlikely to use them to transport anything as sensitive and as prized as a nuclear or radiological device. It is far more likely that such weapons if used would either be assembled inside the target country using as many locally available components as possible, or brought in using small craft.[67] As the head of the US Domestic Nuclear Detection Office remarked in 2007: 'giving up a nuclear device, putting it in a container and letting it float around the world for a couple of weeks is probably folly'. He also observed that more attention needed to be devoted to the threat from what he termed 'non-port of entry venues' such as unguarded stretches of coastline or land border.[68]

Along with the practical obstacles to using freight containers to deliver weapons of this kind, the international security regime has probably also played a role in minimising threats in this area. The Proliferation Security Initiative (PSI) was launched at the instigation of the US at the G8 summit in Poland in May 2003 with the purpose of preventing the proliferation of nuclear, chemical and biological weapons and materials. The PSI requires that participating states enact domestic laws regarding interdiction and seizure, and work to ensure that their national facilities are not used for the transfer of illicit weapon cargoes. Though many states expressed scepticism of the PSI initially (and some still do), over 80 states have now endorsed its original principles, such that the initiative has become a widely accepted counter-proliferation tool. Its implementation in a maritime context has been broadly successful, to the point where it is possible to argue that it has 'effectively protected most of the world's shipping from [involvement in] proliferation'.[69]

Transport of operatives and supplies

Around 90% of the world's trade moves by sea for some portion of its journey. Although the proportion of terrorism-related materials that travel by boat or ship is unknown, it is reasonable to assume that terrorist groups and their supporters are making similarly extensive use of the sea to transport operatives, arms and money. We know that Libya supplied arms to the Provisional IRA by sea,[70] that Iran sent Palestinian fighters arms for the second intifada by boat,[71] and al-Qaeda is believed to have transported the explosives used in the East African embassy bombings by sea.[72] Palestinian insurgents continue to transport arms over water, despite a number of successful interceptions.[73]

Because of their size it is easier to hide illicit cargo on board ships than it is on a land-based form of transport, and the principle of free navigation discourages high-seas interception. So while the possibility of a WMD being transported in a freight container may be remote, the probability that terrorists do use the container system and the maritime transport system in general to transport supplies justifies many of the changes made to port and supply-chain security since 2001, notably those contained in the IMO's International Ship and Port Facility Security Code. Alongside procedural improvements, a counter-terrorism presence at sea is also valuable. NATO's *Operation Active Endeavour*, set up in October 2001, patrols the eastern Mediterranean with the aim of detecting terrorists and insurgents, principally al-Qaeda, using ships to move men and materiel, and CTF 150, along with two other Coalition task forces, continues to patrol the Arabian Sea.

Terrorist 'navies' and 'proto-navies'

Naval, or 'proto-naval', activity has been undertaken by the LTTE and attempted by some anti-Israel groups, principally Fatah, and, to a lesser extent, Hizbullah. The LTTE's dependence on the sea for much of its movement and supply needs has meant that the Sea Tigers have, in the course of escorting supply boats, been compelled to engage in running battles with SLN ships, giving rise to the development of a maritime capacity approaching that of a navy, which allows them to operate sea control and trade defence missions that, although limited, present enough of a threat to worry India as well as Sri Lanka.[74] The Tigers even possess a rudimentary amphibious capability.[75]

The LTTE also has its own logistical fleet, known informally as the 'Sea Pigeons'.[76] Estimates of how many ocean-going cargo ships are operating at any one time vary between nine and 15, and a figure of 11 is the most frequently cited.[77] These vessels do not carry LTTE supplies exclusively; such supplies are hidden amongst much larger volumes of legitimate cargo. The vessels are also used to smuggle arms and clandestine migrants,[78] and a role in drug smuggling is strongly suspected. In an address to the IISS's Shangri-La Dialogue in 2007, Sri Lankan Foreign Minister Rohitha Bogollagama claimed that 'LTTE ships have been used to provide alternate supply channels to other groups and crime syndicates in the region for their arms, human smuggling and drug trafficking activities'.[79]

Palestinian insurgents' naval capacity was initiated in 1967 with the creation, at a pan-Arab summit immediately prior to the Six Day War, of a 'Palestinian Arab Navy'.[80] Terrorism analyst Samuel Katz has argued that with most of the Jordan valley sealed, the Syrian and Lebanese borders well protected and Sinai occupied, the sea was virtually the Palestinians' only option. A regular clandestine ferry route was established between Beirut and Gaza. Fishermen and smugglers were recruited, and a small body of combat swimmers and commandos established. Fatah reportedly amassed vessels ranging from 150 to 500 tonnes, based in Cyprus and the Lebanese port of Tripoli. These functioned as mother ships to support small craft (usually *Zodiacs*) that were used to land supplies of weapons, saboteurs and raiding parties on the Israeli coast.[81] In 1978, when the IDF undertook *Operation Litani*, its limited invasion of southern Lebanon, it uncovered an extensive naval infrastructure of workshops and weapons stores. It found one-man mini-submarines, small reconnaissance boats (apparently supplied by Libya), fibreglass speedboats equipped with machine guns, *Zodiacs*, diving gear, navigation devices and rafts fitted with multiple *Katyusha*-122 rocket launchers. Documents seized revealed that Fatah was trying to buy small warships from the Soviet Union, Arab navies and on the black market.[82] Following the signing of the Oslo Accords in 1993 much of Fatah's maritime capacity, including officers and men, was transferred to the newly formed Palestinian Authority coast guard.

Between 2001 and 2003, reports appeared in the Western press of an 'al-Qaeda fleet'.[83] These reports, which seem to have been based on suspicions about shipping companies that function as fronts for illicit activities, are now largely discounted; maritime expert Charles Dragonette is convinced that they had 'little foundation in reality'.[84] Nonetheless, there is no disputing that al-Qaeda and its affiliates have easy access to shipping on the commercial market for transport purposes (as does any adequately funded terrorist organisation).

Terrorism at sea: principal actors

Relatively few terrorist groups have operated at sea. Some, including ETA and some Chechen organisations,[85] have done so occasionally and opportunistically, while others have made attempts at maritime operations for a period, then stopped. The Provisional IRA tried at various points to launch a coherent maritime campaign, but without success, and anti-Castro Cuban groups operated at sea intermittently for nearly two decades, also without achieving substantial success, before giving up.

Only a handful of groups using terrorism have developed what could be described as a maritime capability, mounting either a sustained maritime campaign or using maritime assets to support their activities on land, or both. These organisations are worth discussing in more detail.

GAM

GAM (the Free Aceh Movement) began fighting for Acehnese independence from Indonesia in 1976. Its maritime arm was developed as a matter of necessity, given Aceh's geography. The organisation depended heavily on gun-running, mainly from southern Thailand.[86] It also raised money through the capture and ransom of crews from vessels at the northern end of the Malacca Strait.[87] GAM was severely depleted practically and psychologically by the destruction and loss of manpower caused by the 2004 tsunami, and entered into ceasefire negotiations with the Jakarta government soon after the disaster.[88]

The MNLF and MILF

The MNLF is an Islamist insurgent organisation, begun in the 1970s to fight for an independent nation for the Moro ethnic minority in the Philippines.[89] It has been in a ceasefire agreement with the Manila government since 1996, but it appears to have benefited from external arms supplies over the course of its existence, reputedly from China and a number of Arab states, notably Libya.

However, immediately before and for some time after it signed the 1976 Tripoli peace agreement with the Philippines government (which quickly soured), foreign assistance to the MNLF diminished, and it extorted money from local fishermen and hijacked ships for publicity and to earn money from ransom payments. It is believed to be responsible for the hijack of the *Suehiro Maru* near Manila in 1975 and the attack on the *Don Carlos* in 1978 using four speedboats. It also mounted two attacks in 1982 on inter-island ferries to extort money from the owners.

MILF, which broke away from the MNLF in 1972, is currently the largest Islamist insurgent group in the Philippines, with an estimated membership of 10–12,000.[90] Though it has undertaken less maritime activity than the MNLF, it is linked to an attack on the ferry *Our Lady Mediatrix* in 2000 and one on a wharf in Davao City in 2003 where two inter-island ferries were moored, which killed 16 people and injured 55.

The ASG

The ASG started life as a separatist Islamist organisation among the Tausug people indigenous to the Sulu archipelago in the Philippines, but after the death of its founder Abdurajak Janjalani in December 1998, it fractured into two violent gangs. One was based on the island of Basilan at the top of the archipelago under the leadership of Janjalani's brother. The other, based on Jolo, in the middle of the Sulu chain, and led by another gangster, 'Commander Robot', pursued largely criminal activities, to the apparent detriment of the group's ostensible political objectives.[91]

Since the split, both groups within the ASG have mounted attacks at sea, primarily to raise funds, although how much for the cause and how much for the personal gain of the group's leaders is difficult to determine. An ASG speciality has been coastal raiding. ASG operatives attacked the predominantly Christian town of Ipil in 1995 using tactics similar to those used by anti-Israel groups. The group has also successfully undertaken two major raids on resorts with the aim of kidnapping mostly Westerners for ransom: in Sabah, Malaysia in 2000 and in Palawan in the Philippines in 2001.

The ASG's attack on the inter-island *SuperFerry 14* in 2004 in which 116 people died, reportedly undertaken because the ferry operator refused to accede to a ransom demand, dramatically demonstrated the vulnerability of open-access maritime transport.

The LTTE

The LTTE became the dominant militant Tamil separatist group in Sri Lanka in 1987, when it gained effective control of the Jaffna peninsula in the north, and much of the east coast. From the beginning it recognised that a maritime capability was essential. Velupillai Prabhakaran made this clear when he reportedly declared that 'geographically the security of Tamil Eelam [the Tamil nation] is interlinked with that of its seas. It is only when we are strong on the seas and break the dominance the enemy now has that we will be able to retain the land areas we liberated and drive our enemies from our homeland.'[92]

When the insurgency began, the LTTE's rear base area was across the Palk Strait from Sri Lanka in the Indian state of Tamil Nadu.[93] Contact between base area and combat zone was maintained with fast dinghies and slower fishing vessels, but the SLN inflicted heavy losses on both types of craft.[94] In response, the Sea Tigers were formed in 1984. As it has developed from being an essentially defensive organisation to being one that conducts sea control, supply and amphibious support operations from the strait and around the northern and eastern coasts of the island, the Sea Tigers force has become the most capable and tactically astute of all seaborne insurgency groups. Since its inception it has destroyed between a third and a half of the SLN's coastal fleet and in 2000 played a crucial role in the surrender of Sri Lankan government forces on the Jaffna peninsula.[95] The Sea Tigers have shown what maritime insurgents can achieve if they pursue their goals with determination, innovation and, indeed, a willingness to engage in suicide operations. Additionally, the Sea Pigeons fleet bolsters the LTTE's considerable presence at sea.

Other insurgent and terrorist groups, such as al-Qaeda, have studied the LTTE's maritime operations and learned from them; the attack on the USS *Cole* bears marked similarities to previous Sea Tiger attacks on SLN vessels.[96] Counter-terrorism experts also recognise the organisation's achievements. Bahukutumbi Raman, a strategic analyst and the former head of the Indian intelligence service's counter-terrorism division, rates the LTTE as the 'most intelligent and futuristic-thinking [sic] terrorist organisation in the world'; its leaders, according to Vijay Sakhuja, have 'tremendous capacity and vision'.[97] In addition to being the only insurgent organisation that effectively has its own navy and air force, it was also able to hijack the *Intelsat*-12 satellite for over two years to transmit its own news programmes from 2005 to 2007. It apparently regards the loss of access as only a temporary setback.[98]

Anti-Israel groups

Since 11 September, maritime analysts have tended to focus on the possibility of more attacks like those on the *Cole* and *Limburg*, and the potential for terrorist assaults in the Strait of Malacca, neglecting the maritime aspect of the long-running conflict between Israel and various, primarily Palestinian, insurgent groups. The Israel–Palestine conflict has had a substantial maritime dimension ever since anti-Israel groups began operating at sea in 1966–67. Groups have aimed to exploit Israel's maritime flank to land arms and raiding parties, to take hostages to be exchanged for prisoners held by Israel, and to launch attacks, mostly on the IDF Navy. Between April 1985 and early 1987, the navy and other elements of the IDF were able to deny Palestinian insurgents access to the Israeli coast, and intercepted several consignments of arms and a number of senior Fatah commanders in transit.[99] The navy itself became a target for attacks partly due to its continuing success in such ventures.

Palestinian terrorist groups have made numerous attempts to bring arms into Israel using ships: the *Santorini* (2001), the *Karine A* (2002) and the *Abu Hassan* (2003) were intercepted successfully, but other attempts may well have succeeded. A single vessel carrying half a tonne of explosives can easily be lost among the 400–600 Palestinian fishing boats that operate off the Gaza Strip on most nights.

The newer Islamist groups Hamas and Palestinian Islamic Jihad have sought to engage IDF vessels more aggressively than did Fatah. Hamas has twice attempted to attack Israeli naval vessels, in 2000 and again in 2002. Both groups have mounted a number of attacks using suicide bombers, or deception, or both. Deception techniques have become a regular feature of attacks: booby-trapped life rafts and fishing boats have exploded when IDF Navy vessels have tried to inspect them.[100] Swimmers have also been used frequently, both to infiltrate coastal areas and to transport arms from Egypt into Gaza.[101]

Since 2000, the element of the maritime conflict that has warranted closest attention is the connection between Lebanon-based Hizbullah and Iran. Over this period, Iran has reinforced Hizbullah's maritime capability. A senior Iranian officer claimed in 2006 that Hizbullah had a submarine unit and a 'naval commando unit that operates Chinese-manufactured speed boats capable of targeting the Israeli navy'.[102] It is possible, given its access to substantial Iranian support, and its global reach (it has cells on several continents and has probably been responsible for attacks on land in Argentina and for planned attacks on maritime targets in Singapore)[103] that Hizbullah could in the future become a more formidable maritime adversary than the Sea Tigers, al-Qaeda or any other terrorist group.

Nicaraguan Contras

In 1983, the Contras, armed opponents of Nicaragua's Sandinista government, acting in many instances under US guidance, launched a maritime campaign directed at the Nicaraguan economy. In 1984 they increased the pressure on the government by mining all of the country's ports, repelling foreign trading vessels just at the point when major consignments of Nicaragua's main export, agricultural products, were to be shipped overseas, with grave consequences for the economy and the government's standing within the country. As maritime law expert Samuel Pyeatt Menefee comments: 'Similar in nature to Russian activity during the Korean

War and to the mining of the Red Sea ... the Contra mining campaign and related harbour attacks show what is possible for an insurrectionary force to accomplish with assistance from an involved state'.[104]

Al-Qaeda and its affiliates

Though in the past few years al-Qaeda's planning focus has been almost exclusively on land, maritime operations have been a largely successful element of the organisation's repertoire, partly due to the dynamism of Abd al-Rahim al-Nashiri. While evidence given to a tribunal at Guantanamo Bay in March 2007 cast some doubt over the extent to which al-Nashiri directed the highest-profile of al-Qaeda's attacks at sea,[105] he retains his status as the organisation's principal maritime strategist.

Given his involvement in major attacks such at the 1998 East African embassy bombings, it is reasonable to suppose that al-Nashiri would have attempted to fuse his maritime and mass-casualty experience had he not been captured in 2002. Nonetheless, while he was free, his focus was on iconic targets such as the *Cole*, and, to a lesser extent, economic ones, such as tankers. Al-Nashiri's favoured mode of assault was suicide attacks on stationary or near-stationary targets and, like all al-Qaeda commanders, he laid great stress on extensive pre-attack surveillance.[106] He appeared to recognise the importance of chokepoints, although it is likely that his focus here was primarily on staging attacks with a strong visual impact, as opposed to creating ones with mainly economic or logistical consequences. A visual impact was more likely to be achieved by leaving a ship or several ships burning and disabled in a narrow waterway than by attacking them out on the open ocean.

How successful is maritime terrorism?

The *Achille Lauro* hijack and al-Qaeda's assaults on the *Cole* and the *Limburg* briefly caught Western media attention and, rather more enduringly, that of governments and the maritime industry. But as a rule, when attacks have been mounted at sea, the results in terms of publicity have been limited. That terrorists themselves recognise this is shown by the fact that so few have taken place. The special challenges of the sea make attacks major enough to be the focus of media and governments difficult to accomplish. The sinking of a large cruise ship or ferry, killing thousands of Westerners, the bombing of a warship, the successful delivery of a nuclear or radiological device to a major port, or the execution of multiple and harmful attacks on the world's maritime transport system are all scenarios that are less easily brought about than equivalent events on land.

Most terrorists are not used to the sea. Training and gaining experience in navigation, coastal piloting and ship handling takes time, even where terrorists are able to draw on a maritime tradition. Any operation must take account of tidal movement, currents, wind, sea state, visibility, proximity to land, underwater obstacles and the often unpredictable course changes of other boats.[107] Knowledge of local sea conditions and shipping practices is critical. Terrorists usually like to place targets under intense, long-term surveillance, and to map out their attack patterns. These are sensible preparatory methods for the unpredictable marine environment, but there are fewer places where it is possible to loiter discreetly at sea than there are on land. Testing weapons and practising an attack run is also difficult, for similar reasons. Terrorism analyst Bruce Hoffman believes that many terrorists operating today prefer not to undertake complex attacks that demand sophisticated planning and execution,[108] but operating at sea usually necessitates sophisticated methods, and specialist knowledge, skills and equipment are needed for attacks on ships. Some analysts have suggested that as so many maritime targets are poorly secured they are likely to attract attention from terrorists.[109] There certainly are plenty of soft targets at sea, but in general they have not been sufficiently accessible, given the difficulties outlined, to displace land targets in the hierarchy of terrorist preferences.

Consequently maritime terrorism has posed a threat to a very modest number of countries, chiefly Israel, Sri Lanka, the Philippines, Yemen, Nicaragua and what was once the Spanish Sahara. Furthermore, except in the case of Sri Lanka, these threats have been largely peripheral. Nevertheless, it is worth reviewing such threats as do exist in terms of potential targets and methods.

The most prominent iconic targets at sea, warships, remain vulnerable to small boat attacks, but they are for the most part more secure now than they were before the attack on the *Cole*. Causing mass casualties on land is clearly within the terrorist compass, but at sea it is more difficult. Large concentrations of people are only found at sea on board cruise liners and ferries. Ferries, like all open-access means of transport, do remain highly vulnerable. As for cruise ships, since security measures designed to prevent internal seizure were implemented, such as the screening of passengers and their luggage, a terrorist group's most practical option has been to crash a boat manned by a suicide bomber into the ship's side, but though this has been planned it has not as yet been attempted.

Though there is a minor threat in this context, large ships are usually much more difficult to blow up than aircraft, and while in theory large ships are usable as weapons with which to attack ports or other ships, the practical obstacles are considerable. Fixed economic targets at sea such as oil and gas platforms, terminals and pipelines are more vulnerable than ships, particularly because of the material they handle, but the difficulties involved in overcoming security measures and negotiating the sea itself in order to launch an attack are numerous. No terrorist assault on a fixed installation at sea has yet succeeded.

There is also the option of raiding fixed land targets from the sea. The Sea Tigers have conducted what are in effect full-scale amphibious assaults, while some anti-Israel groups and MILF and the ASG in the Philippines have launched smaller-scale raids to kill people or take hostages. As there are many economic and infrastructure targets such as power stations, oil terminals and refineries, and mass-casualty targets such as shopping malls, hotels and exposed beaches readily accessible from the sea, it is surprising that raids have not been launched more frequently, especially in view of the fact that, as few law enforcement bodies have a maritime capability, the raiders would probably be able to escape relatively easily.

Finally, the most significant threat posed by terrorists at sea, that of an assault from an IED-equipped small boat, is lesser than its land equivalent. Driving an explosive-laden boat into even a fixed target is unlikely to have even the effect that driving an explosive-laden car into a building might. Roads are static; the surface of the sea is not. If the target is moving as well as the attacker, then it is even more difficult to take accurate aim.[110]

It is important not to exaggerate the threat from maritime terrorism. As the United Kingdom's First Sea Lord and Chief of the Naval Staff between 2002 and 2006, Admiral Sir Alan West warned that maritime terrorism was 'a clear and present danger' that could 'potentially cripple global trade and have grave knock-on effects on developed economies'.[111] He was not alone in making such an assessment. But this is surely an overestimation of the threat. For the reasons discussed above, launching attacks on maritime targets presents particular problems such that the option of perpetrating an equivalent act on land will in the majority of cases be more attractive.[112]

Discussion of maritime terrorism in the media, the academy and intelligence agencies can suffer from circularity, whereby analysts and commentators discuss possible scenarios, terrorists listen, analysts then pick up chatter that reflects their speculations, and take it to be proof that their suspicions were correct.[113] Any threat that maritime terrorism presents to international security or to the international flow of people and goods – as distinct from the threats it poses to specific localities – remains at a low level, at least for now.

CHAPTER THREE

Assessing the Threat

Viewed in isolation from other kinds of maritime disorder and corruption on land, pirate attacks are currently a localised problem. They have a negligible effect on world trade and the movement of people. Similarly, on its own, maritime terrorism does not present a major threat. The number of incidents is insignificant, not even worth a separate mention in the US State Department's *Patterns of Global Terrorism* reports. So why should either phenomenon be regarded as a threat to international security? Do we need in addition to confront a more generalised problem of maritime disorder?

Maritime disorder and initiatives for tackling it

Disorder at sea has always existed. The maritime world is anarchic and where order has been present it has been kept by a hegemon; it has depended on the self-interest of an imperial or global power or powers to enforce it, whether alone or with the help of regional allies. In the absence of such a power or powers, seafarers have generally been subject to the depredations of criminal pirates or state-sponsored privateers.

An anarchic state obtains on the high seas in particular. In the case of failed states (such as Somalia) or weak states (such as Sierra Leone and Papua New Guinea), the absence of regulation and law enforcement may extend right up to the coast.[1] Even in the case of slightly stronger states (such as Indonesia, the Philippines and Bangladesh), it may extend to the coast in areas away from major population centres and, because of inadequate law enforcement or corruption, can effectively include major ports – Chittagong in Bangladesh and Lagos in Nigeria are clear examples.

Faced with this comparatively unregulated and semi-anarchic realm, navies and coast guards have devised strategies designed to gain greater understanding of the threats, criminal and political, that thrive there. Maritime Domain Awareness (MDA) is an example of such a strategy. MDA, which was developed by the US Coast Guard, has two main elements: surveillance of activities at sea; and intelligence-gathering on the background to the movements and presences identified. Since 11 September, the focus of MDA has included potentially all ship and boat movements, based on the recognition that any illegal activity at sea can have security implications.[2] The aim is to pool vast quantities of data on illicit activities at sea from a wide variety of sources, for instance the data on ship movements collected by Lloyds Maritime Intelligence Unit, and 'fuse' them in a common format which can then be made accessible to interested parties, subject to classification, in what is known as a 'common operating picture' (renamed more recently a 'user-defined operating picture').

The scheme is complex, and it has yet to be seen how it will function when fully elaborated. The successful achievement of its aim of building a picture of threats at sea that is sufficiently clear to be acted on will depend on overcoming a number of substantial technical and procedural problems. Furthermore, care must be taken that the surveillance element of the initiative does not take precedence over intelligence, which it has at times threatened to do. MDA is an ambitious project whose scale, and the difficulties it faces, illustrate the immensity of the challenge posed by the ever-changing character of illicit maritime activity.

A wider context in which MDA might be applied was put forward in 2006, when Admiral Mullen, Chief of Naval Operations for the US Navy, called for the creation of a 'thousand-ship navy' (TSN). The idea behind TSN was that navies and other users of the sea such as shipping companies should, regardless of their capabilities or technical sophistication, work to promote global maritime security by cooperating to confront common problems such as arms smuggling and terrorism.[3] The concept, which is now also referred to as the 'Global Maritime Partnership', had been first outlined the year before Mullen's statement, in an article published in *Proceedings*, in which pirates, human traffickers, drug smugglers and other organised criminals were identified as being amongst the transnational threats that the power of concerned states and maritime organisations should be harnessed to confront.[4]

What exactly TSN might mean in practice has been difficult to determine, partly because the US Navy has been at pains to stress the voluntary nature of any association and so has avoided explicit prescriptions of what it ought to cover. In broad terms, however, the aim is to encourage information-sharing; to achieve a common awareness of the quantity and types of illicit maritime activity at sea in order that maritime security assets (essentially ships and aircraft) may be positioned to deter such activity and disrupt criminal and terrorist use of the sea. As most navies currently lack the capacity to act on such information effectively, the concept also extends to capacity-building and the suggestion has been made that major navies, the US Navy in particular, should provide support and assistance in this context. This has met with a mixed reception, as although the US Navy has been at pains to emphasise its awareness of other nations' sovereignty, it has nevertheless met with accusations of playing what one commentator has called 'globo-cop' in the maritime arena.[5]

MDA and TSN are both promising, but as yet largely unrealised, elements of a security regime that is faced with a problem of maritime disorder that is growing rapidly, as all kinds of exploitation of the sea intensify and illicit activity keeps pace. In this context, those who argue that the overall security of the maritime world can be ensured by multilateral treaties or regimes in anything other than a limited or temporary sense, without the leadership of a hegemonic power, have scant evidence upon which to base their faith.

The sea today

Pressures on the sea have been mounting steadily since 1945. Since the end of the Cold War, the incidence of piracy has increased, both the transportation of legitimate goods and the smuggling of drugs, arms, natural resources, slaves and other illegal migrants by sea has increased substantially, and fish stocks have been depleted, in some areas almost to exhaustion. Exploitation of the sea has now reached unprecedented levels, driven by the rapidly rising demand for resources and living space on land, due to population growth and environmental degradation. States and corporations are turning to the sea more than ever before for energy, in the form of offshore oil and gas and structures that capture wind or tidal power, and for minerals, drinking water distilled from the sea, and waste disposal. The sea is also being exploited more than ever before for food, both from increasingly depleted fish stocks and from fish farmed in sheltered waters. Added to these pressures is the exploitation of coastal areas by the wealthy portion of the world's population for tourism and leisure, including the building of structures on the sea itself, such as those seen currently in South Pacific island lagoons and the 'palm island' developments in Dubai. This is a trend that is likely to continue, as the proportion of the world's population able to afford such privileges grows. Greater economic activity will create more targets for maritime crime and terrorism. In the commercial sphere, as the trend for using fewer, and larger, cargo ships in a smaller number of giant ports continues (while the number of narrow chokepoints remains constant), and the quantity of goods in transit grows, opportunities for successful criminal interdiction will increase.

As seaward movements intensify, and coastal activity increases, climate change is likely simultaneously to cause the sea to encroach upon the land. These opposing pressures mean that the sea will become more contested in the future.[6] Resource depletion and the loss of productive land to environmental damage will increase the economic and political pressure on the littorals and may well make conflict more likely. Currently, international law in the form of UNCLOS sets the limits of territorial seas and determines the rights of states within EEZs, thereby imposing some degree of order on coastal regions. UNCLOS was the product of a compromise between the often conflicting interests of coastal states and maritime powers, and there is a danger that in the future political pressures exerted by seaward migration and rising sea levels, and the attendant environmental and security concerns, could create rifts between states such that UNCLOS is able to exert less and less force in practice, perhaps even to the point that it fractures.

This context of an increasingly pressured and potentially semi-lawless and chaotic environment is the one in which possible developments in maritime criminality and terror must be assessed.[7] Upward trends in population and economic activity and the concomitant rising demand for marine resources could aggravate three kinds of threat and vulnerability in particular: criminality and criminal–terrorist cooperation; weaknesses in the international trade system, and the threat of maritime insurgency.

Criminality and criminal–terrorist cooperation

Despite their different goals, terrorists and criminals in general, if not usually pirates in particular, have on occasion found reason to work together. Terrorists and insurgents have always committed other crimes when necessary, usually in order to secure funds, but in the past they rarely sought out direct or regular contact with criminals; interestingly, increasing criminality was often a sign that a group was in decline. This has changed. Terrorists and insurgents, faced with reduced state sponsorship following the end of the Cold War and the inception of the 'global war on terror', both of which have made it far more difficult for them to raise funds and transfer money by legal or quasi-legal means, have been turning to crime, and criminal accomplices, more readily and at an earlier stage in their evolution.

Although individual attacks can be mounted relatively cheaply, there are the running costs of a terrorist network to be taken into account as well when considering terrorist expenditure, and, though hardly extravagant, these nevertheless impose funding demands. In 2004 the secretary-general of Interpol, Ronald Noble, estimated that only 10% of al-Qaeda's estimated 2001 expenditure of $30–$50 million went on attacks; the rest was used to run the organisation.[8] With less state sponsorship available, terrorist groups have had to finance themselves through private benefactors and a variety of criminal activities, including siphoning off funds from legitimate businesses, acquiring illicit funding through charity organisations, dealing in counterfeit goods, drug trafficking, extortion and bank robbery.[9]

In the first instance, terrorists are still most likely to turn to other terrorists for help: they recognise that cooperating with other kinds of criminals exposes them to security risks.[10] But other terrorists will not always have the resources needed, and sometimes criminal organisations will hold attractions in addition to financial ones. In his 2004 report for the US Congressional Research Service on the links between terrorism and drugs, policy analyst Mark Kleiman lists four reasons why criminals in the drug trade and terrorists might cooperate: for money; to create chaos and instability in the countries where drugs are grown and through which they are moved; to encourage a climate in which corruption is acceptable and intimidation is unopposed; and to provide cover and a common infra-structure for their joint and separate activities.[11] FARC in Colombia, the United Wa State Army in Myanmar and, in a different way, al-Qaeda and the Taliban in Afghanistan, have all worked with criminals, mainly those involved in the drug trade, probably for the reasons listed. The LTTE's Sea Tigers have worked with Arakanese smugglers in Myanmar and northeast India,[12] transported supplies for arms traders and aided people traffick-ers. Unspecified terrorist groups have in the past couple of decades made increasing use of the human smuggling routes through the Mediterranean to bring operatives into Europe, and bought arms and documents from smugglers and forgers. In the Philippines MILF and the ASG have connec-tions with the 'Pentagon' gang of kidnappers.[13]

In some contexts the relationship between terrorist and common criminals becomes closer than one based on sporadic cooperation and

Figure 6 **Terrorists and common criminals: cooperation, convergence and transformation**[14]	
Type of relationship	**Definition**
Cooperation	A variety of mutually beneficial contacts, ranging from the provision of arms, documents and safe houses through to the exchange of skills, intelligence and other services
Convergence	Terrorist and criminal groups form partnerships to exploit long- to medium-term criminal opportunities for their mutual benefit, without abandoning their separate identities
Transformation	Terrorist group adapts itself so that it can carry out criminal activities without outside support

knowledge-sharing, and insurgent groups can effectively converge with, or even transform into, criminal organisations (see Figure 6). The relationship between the Taliban and al-Qaeda and drug traffickers in Afghanistan has at times been one of near-convergence, and FARC is an example of an organisation that has practically transformed into a criminal group, having had its origins in insurgent activity.

While these processes do not relate directly to the sea, in a busier and even less regulated maritime world, where there may as a result be more opportunities for criminals of all kinds to act with impunity in the future, such functional relationships between networks of common criminals and insurgents using terrorism could thrive and their combined skills and resources could present greater challenges to maritime security.[15]

The threat to trade: the vulnerability of the commercial maritime transport system

Though the difficulties involved make the delivery of a WMD device using the international container system and 'spectacular' terror attacks on ports or chokepoints using large ships unlikely, the international commercial maritime transport system is still relatively 'soft' in spite of the security precautions implemented since 2001, and therefore has its attractions as a terrorist target. (It is also in theory vulnerable to disruption from un-intended blockages of vital waterways caused by pirate attacks.)

There are multiple entry points to the system, many of them in weak states, but above all it is the character of the system itself, with its strict timetables, short turn-around times, narrow financial margins, widespread dependence on information technology and sensitivity to fluctuations in shareholder and consumer confidence that makes it vulnerable to disruption.[16]

Over a hundred years ago, American sea power theorist Alfred Thayer Mahan called the sea the 'great highway',[17] and observed that the global trading system that used it was delicate. In many ways, it is even more delicate now than it was then. According to the World Bank, global maritime trade amounted to 21,480bn ton-miles in 1999 and was expected to grow to 35,000bn ton-miles by 2010 and 41,800bn ton-miles by 2014.[18] Greater volumes are being carried with greater efficiency than before. Greater efficiency is being achieved through greater concentration. Redundancy has been sacrificed, as bigger and bigger ships that can only dock at a small number of giant 'hub' ports become the favoured goods carriers.[19] Buffer stocks have been stripped away to save money. Half a century without a world war, the cargo integrity that came with containerisation, better global communications and weather forecasting, and a decline in piracy for most of the twentieth century from its highs in the eighteenth and nineteenth combined to encourage shippers, insurers and maritime organisations to expect the system to run smoothly and to assess threats in terms of the risk of accidents, not the risk of attack. Consequently the system is in some ways quite unprepared for deliberate disruption, and, though efficient, is also rather brittle. The vulnerability of consumer and shareholder confidence to setbacks and delays is an illustration of this.

Though the sensitivity of markets vary – attacks on oil installations, for instance, have not to date had lasting effects on prices[20] – sensitivity could become vulnerability if attacks were persistent and were amplified by a determined information campaign. The cumulative loss of confidence in the system or in its constituent parts to deliver goods reliably that might result from extensive terrorist disruption would be reflected in rising prices, particularly energy and commodity prices and rates for insurance and shipping, which would affect productivity.[21] The economic effects of any serious disturbance could be felt globally and states, particularly weaker states, might be faced with instability if food and fuel supplies were severely affected or prices rose dramatically.

The terrorism-related risks that most concern marine insurers currently are pollution, the blockage of a chokepoint such that shipping is forced to make a time-consuming diversion, and the closure of a port with significant numbers of ships trapped inside. Other, remoter threats might also be realised. A material like LNG may not be an attractive tool for terrorists on its own, but a supply chain consisting of ships dispersed across the oceans, 200–300 miles apart, departing and arriving at terminals and transiting chokepoints on predictable schedules that are set contractually years in advance could be severely damaged by an attack on an LNG carrier and the threat of more. The prospect of achieving a level of disruption that would send tremors, not only throughout the target economy, but also through all economies dependent on similar supply chains, could whet a terrorist's interest in LNG or another similar resource, despite the practical challenges it presents. Likewise, the detonation of explosive devices in ports or on board ships, though very difficult to achieve, could if successful severely shake confidence in the security of the supply chain and thereby weaken a system which, because it has taken the permanent availability of low-cost security for granted, is constantly seeking efficiencies and to drive down costs.[22]

The international transport system's sensitivity to such attacks is untested but particular aspects of it, such as the 'just-in-time' (JIT) inventory system, appear potentially vulnerable to shocks like terrorist assaults. JIT is now used by many international manufacturers and retailers. It enables components to be delivered to a production line, and products to stores, just at the time they are needed, rather than their being held in stock. Its use over the past two decades has led buyers and sellers to expect more from the transport system that links them. Once the international maritime transport system had succeeded in demonstrating the reliability necessary to make JIT work, user approval grew, and more companies in more countries adopted it. Confidence in JIT having spread, trade increased, as many companies, particularly major transnational corporations, were able to outsource their manufacturing to plants in countries with lower labour costs. Increased confidence led to stockholdings throughout the system falling, dramatically releasing working capital, which, in turn, caused sharp rises in productivity.

Whereas companies used to hold considerable stocks, with JIT they are more prepared to rely on the security of their goods in transit instead; ships have become, in effect, warehouses. If delays were to occur in the system for any reason, it could mean that stockholdings throughout the system would rise again as buyers responded to the increased uncertainty, tying up working capital, space and labour. Productivity would fall. Economic performance would decline, which would erode that elusive economic driver, confidence. Fear of supply-chain failure could have a serious economic impact. A study prepared by David Closs of Michigan State University in 2002 revealed that large US manufacturers held an average of 1.57 months' worth of stock in the early 1990s. By 2001 this had fallen to 1.36 months' worth. Following 11 September, Closs expected this to increase to 1.43 months' worth in 2002. In other words, in just one year, the fear of terrorist disruption might have halved the logistic-chain productivity gains made over the previous decade and could have added between $50 and $80bn to US business costs. These costs would, moreover, have been in addition to the new supply-chain security measures put in place since the 11 September attacks that are estimated to cost the US economy alone $65bn annually.[23] That this scenario did not in fact come about is attributable to other, benign, economic factors, including lower demand for fuel.[24] A future sudden increase in stockholdings in response to a crisis cannot be ruled out, however, particularly in circumstances where positive countervailing factors are absent.

Such potential weaknesses in the commercial maritime transport system demand serious attention. As the volume of trade transported by sea increases, and the sea's resources are exploited with greater intensity, the system's vulnerabilities to disruption, including from terror attacks, will have correspondingly greater implications for the world's economy and security.

Occasionally, however, the system's sensitivity to disruption can be beneficial. In autumn 2005, the Joint War Committee (JWC) of Lloyd's designated the Malacca Strait an area of 'Perceived Enhanced Risk' (PER), because of concerns about maritime disorder in the strait, including piracy and the risk of terrorism. This met with vehement protest from maritime analysts, ship-owners and politicians in the region. The designation was rescinded in August 2006 but it appears to have had a greater positive effect on the security of the strait than most of the resolutions passed by international and regional bodies for decades, and as much as the 2004 US proposal to establish an RMSI and the political pressure exerted by Japan over the previous two decades.[25] The JWC's action put an economic price on piracy, one that the littoral governments could neither ignore nor disguise. Concern that the strait might be 're-listed' has meant that measures that might never otherwise have been agreed, or if agreed never or only partially implemented, or if implemented not funded adequately or sustained, are likely to be kept in place until they have been shown to have brought the threat from disorder in the strait under control.[26]

Port and supply-chain security

Some of the system's vulnerabilities can be addressed at the level of port and supply-chain security arrangements. These can be viewed in terms of two principal components, regulatory (or procedural) security and operational security. Broadly speaking, there are two types of regulatory measure: those that aim to reduce the vulnerabilities of ports and the vessels operating within them; and those that aim to secure the cargo moving through ports by addressing the integrity of the supply chain.[27] Operational security measures are largely intelligence led. Terrorists seek to compensate for their comparative lack of resources by using long-term reconnaissance to identify their targets' regular patterns of behaviour. Operational security activities aim to inject uncertainty into such plans, mainly by making unexpected and abrupt alterations to the processes the reconnaissance seeks to monitor.

Port and supply-chain security could be reinforced by a move away from proliferating layers of regulatory security involving detection equipment of sometimes questionable accuracy. Regulatory methods are essentially passive, and as such run the risk of handing the initiative to the terrorist. Operational methods are more active and, when well executed, are more likely to retain the initiative in the hands of the defenders of security by redefining the context in which terrorists operate. The different strands of security practice ought to complement one another, and the system would benefit from a shift in the balance between them, such that effective operational methods play a greater role than they have done in recent years. To work well, security measures should in addition not only be intelligence led; mobile forces should also be flexibly deployed, for instance by periodically flooding areas with security personnel, in order to keep terrorists' level of uncertainty high.

There must also be a cultural change in the system: the pre-eminent importance of security must become as ingrained in the thinking of everyone working in the supply chain as that of workplace safety has over the past two decades. Effecting this change will not be easy and will probably take several years. Finally, societies need to become more resilient. In addition to the preparation by security forces of strategies, plans and resources to minimise damage and disruption in the event of a successful attack, there needs to be a recognition by the public that terrorists may still succeed in executing attacks. International 'confidence' must become less fragile and attempts must be made to manage the shock and control the fear upon which terrorists depend.

Maritime insurgency

Prognoses of the future of maritime terrorism have usually been 'more of the same', but with larger explosions and more deaths. These could prove to be accurate, but we need to ask what would induce insurgent or terrorist groups to invest their limited resources in trying to overcome the manifest functional difficulties of operating at sea.[28]

If – and only if – political circumstances changed on land, terrorists might wish or need to operate more at sea. It is important to explore the possibilities, even those that appear remote: if naval forces and maritime security agencies such as coast guards and marine police fail to prepare for such a shift in terrorist priorities, terrorism at sea could in future have more successes. Two scenarios – an increased use of 'sea bases' by US and possibly other forces, and a major political shift taking place in a coastal region that fortifies terrorist, particularly jihadist, pressures – exemplify the kinds of developments that might lead to an increase in the incidence of maritime insurgency.[29]

The sea base is a US naval concept that took shape in the 1990s as an aspect of changing political circumstances on land, whereby pressures on the US military to minimise its footprint for diplomatic reasons grew and an alternative needed to be found. It was also developed in order to create more secure bases: having a moveable base at sea was thought safer than a static one on shore.[30] Sea bases are designed to be more flexible; ships can be added or withdrawn as and when needed. A sense of how a sea base would operate was provided by the collection of US naval vessels, including a Carrier Strike Group, an Expeditionary Strike Group, maritime pre-positioning ships and a hospital ship that assembled off Aceh in 2005 to provide post-tsunami relief.[31] Elements of the concept are also in operation currently in a number of regions.

As originally conceived, sea bases were not intended for long-term deployments; however, it is possible that the US might have no option but to use a sea base if it needs to support indigenous security forces following a Coalition withdrawal from Iraq. Such a base would need to be positioned either in the northern Persian Gulf or the eastern Mediterranean. Both are narrow seas already well frequented by insurgents. It is possible that such a transfer of key American assets from the land to the sea would give insurgents and terrorists in these regions the incentive to develop a greater maritime attack capability in order to be able to harass or disrupt the operation of the sea base, possibly with state support. Nevertheless, the difficulties of operating at sea that are typically experienced by non-state actors would remain, and the target would have very sophisticated defences. A sea base is less vulnerable than a base on land and it is likely that terrorists would take a long time to amass the maritime expertise necessary to effectively confront one directly, if they were able to at all, but as experience with land bases has shown, the expense and the fatigue induced by uninterruptedly high alert levels reduces military efficiency and discourages reenlistment. The sea base's likely response to such pressures, to retire to deeper water, would increase transit times and costs and possibly impair its effectiveness.

While the maritime terror threat is at present minor, there are indications that insurgent activity is increasing in some coastal regions: the

Indian Navy, for example, is concerned about the threat of 'seaborne terrorist strikes against its vast coastline, including [against] strategic offshore and onshore installations'. According to Chief Admiral Sureesh Mehta, the security situation across the entire Indian Ocean has become 'complex, fluid and significantly challenging', with a 'dramatic increase in asymmetric threats'.[32] Viewing maritime terrorism through a wider lens, the most significant challenge may well come in the future from jihadist groups. One of the distinguishing features of jihadist terrorism is its global outlook. Jihadist organisations such as al-Qaeda are skilled at opening new fronts in their war where they detect opportunity or observe weakness. New instability in a given area, for instance in the maritime 'tri-border' area between northeast Borneo and Mindanao and close to the Sulu and Celebes Seas, where criminal activity and weak law enforcement have created a semi-lawless environment,[33] might allow jihadists to operate with greater freedom than they do at present. If such changes took place in regions where the sea offered significant strategic opportunities, such groups might be inclined to invest in developing a maritime capability to supplement and support their strengthened presence on land, perhaps looking to the LTTE's Sea Tigers as a model. The probable chaotic and under-regulated nature of the maritime environment of the near future would be apt to aid such a development of terrorist capability.

To begin with, the focus would be on developing greater capacity to move cadres, equipment and funds. Though the possibility of jihadist insurgents developing anything more substantial than an enhanced logistical ability at sea might seem remote, time and again terrorist and insurgent organisations have been able to depend on the scepticism of military and other analysts about their capabilities and determination to successfully spring surprises. The attacks of 11 September should have undermined this tendency to underestimate terrorist capabilities; so too should the IDF's experience at the hands of Hizbullah in 2006, when it encountered a sophisticated and elaborate layered defensive system that it had never known existed.[34]

With this experience in mind, we might expect terrorists and insurgents in maritime theatres, emboldened by major successes on land, to build on existing maritime expertise to eventually become able to harass commercial and naval traffic to a degree that severely hindered their free movement, and made certain coastal regions high-risk areas for all kinds of vessel. Such an elaboration of insurgent capability at sea could take place in the eastern Mediterranean, the Horn of Africa (including in Yemen), or in Southeast Asia, anywhere from Mindanao in the Philippines through the Indonesian archipelago to Sumatra, including in southern Thailand. Wherever it took place, this development would represent a serious threat to security beyond that region.

Conclusion: assessing the threat

Though it clearly has the potential to develop, terrorism at sea is currently a minor threat on the international scene. But even absent such changes as outlined above, as the sea becomes a more contested realm, terrorists are, quite simply, presented with more potential targets and opportunity for attacks at sea. In addition, the vulnerabilities of the maritime trading system could magnify and globalise the consequences of any future attacks.

The threat posed by piracy to international trade and shipping security, while it undoubtedly exists (particularly in the form of an inadvertent maritime disaster that could disrupt the tightly programmed schedules of the international transport system), has generally been overstated; the threat it presents to local shipping, fishermen and coastal communities has, however, been underestimated, if not ignored.

A more indirect, yet potentially significant, way in which piracy can in some contexts affect security is by deflecting the attention of intelligence and law enforcement away from terrorist activity. Criminals such as traffickers and pirates do not have to cooperate with terrorists in order to do this; they can help them inadvertently simply by going about their normal business. By operating in a context in which multiple layers of criminal activity are in operation simultaneously in an underworld environment that is difficult for an outsider to penetrate, they can confuse the intelligence picture and make terror activities even harder to discern.

But it is the highly organised form of criminal piracy that deserves the closest attention here. In almost all cases it is a branch of national or transnational organised crime. As such, it is connected to wider criminal activity such as the illicit movement of drugs, counterfeit goods and trafficked people, and fuels the corruption that protects such activity, as well as limiting economic opportunity by imposing the unproductive burden of high security costs on what are generally already fragile economies. This weakens and can destabilise states, a process that can have wider security implications. Admiral Mullen of the US Navy has said that 'piracy … can no longer be viewed as someone else's problem. It is a global threat to security because of its deepening ties to international criminal networks, smuggling of hazardous cargoes, and disruption of vital commerce.'[35] Other maritime crimes, such as smuggling, people trafficking, illegal oil bunkering (in which oil is illicitly extracted from pipelines and sold) and illegal fishing very often also have these wider criminal connections and role in corruption, with similar consequences for stability and security. Maritime strategy experts Kimberley Thachuk and Sam Tangredi have argued that 'corruption is the main vehicle, and likely the most socially damaging activity, by which criminal gangs achieve their aims'.[36]

Both piracy and terrorism are 'grey-area' threats. Peter Chalk defines these as 'threats to the stability of sovereign states [from] non-state actors and non-governmental processes and organisations'.[37] The security threat that confronts most governments today is dynamic, multi-faceted and amorphous. Criminals and terrorists do not have the same objectives and even now as a rule they do not collude, but increasingly their means overlap,[38] as do the effects of their activities, including deepened corruption, increased drug addiction, and organised gang violence (increasingly involving the murder of law enforcement officials), such as has been seen in Mexico, Brazil and some Central American states.

The opportunity for pirates and maritime terrorists to operate is largely created by the failure of weak states to deny them safe havens and free movement at sea (although not exclusively – terrorist attacks have been mounted in the waters of Israel, Turkey and Greece, for example) and the accessibility of potential targets in the waters of such states.[39] As terrorism analyst Martha Crenshaw has observed, 'the most salient political factor in the category of permissive causes is a government's inability or unwillingness to prevent terrorism … The absence of effective security measures is a necessary cause.'[40]

Piracy might be a second-order problem on its own, but in its context of wider criminal networks, it is both cause and symptom of state weakness, which in its turn helps terrorism and organised crime to flourish. Terrorism specialist Brian Michael Jenkins remarks that 'while we should not take piracy as a marker for terrorism, it is a useful indication of the level of security … whatever means [are used] to suppress piracy will have a "knock-on" effect of making the operating environment more difficult for terrorists'.[41] The failure to confront piracy effectively has its consequences. Like those of any crime, incidents of piracy are likely to increase and become more serious if they are not suppressed. As the 'broken windows' theory of policing suggests, serious crime can take root in areas where the small things go unpunished.[42]

What piracy and maritime terrorism reveal – perhaps even more clearly than do organised crime and terrorism on land – is that the divergences between states' responses to common problems are as wide as they have ever been and common cause is difficult to achieve. So long as vulnerable states operate behind inviolable borders, treating their external responsi-bilities as largely theoretical, then their problems, whether they involve piracy, smuggling or terrorism, will affect their neighbours and the ships that pass their coasts. Furthermore, as the sea comes under increasing pres-sure in the coming century, the problem of maritime disorder unfettered by strong authority could extend well beyond the waters of weak states.

NOTES

Introduction

1 'Peril on the Sea', *The Economist*, 4 October 2003, pp. 67–8; Gal Luft and Anne Korin, 'Terrorism Goes to Sea', *Foreign Affairs*, vol. 83, no. 6, November–December 2004, p. 67. For a more accurate contemporary report see Keith Bradsher, 'Attacks on Chemical Ships in Southeast Asia Seem to Be Piracy, Not Terror', *New York Times*, 27 March 2003.

2 Aegis has consistently refused to make the report or even the section dealing with this incident available publicly. Nonetheless, interested agencies appear to have received copies and this quote is from Charles H. Dragonette, 'Maritime Legends', *Bulletin of the Atomic Scientists*, vol. 62, no. 5, September–October 2006, p. 18.

3 Interview with Pottengal Mukundan, director of the International Maritime Bureau (IMB), London, April 2004.

4 Interview with Mukundan, April 2004. Dragonette, 'Lost at Sea' (letter to the editor), *Foreign Affairs*, vol. 84, no. 2, March–April 2005, p. 175; Robert Snodden, 'Piracy and Maritime Terrorism: Naval Responses to Existing and Emerging Threats to the Global Seaborne Economy', in Peter Lehr (ed.), *Violence at Sea: Piracy in the Age of Terrorism* (New York: Routledge, 2006), pp. 231–2.

5 Dragonette, 'Maritime Legends', p. 18.

6 Quoted in Patrick Goodenough, 'Maritime Security Takes Center Stage in SE Asia', CNSNews.com, 29 June 2004, http://www.cnsnews.com/ForeignBureaus/archive/200406/FOR20040629b.html.

7 J.L. Anderson, 'Piracy and World History: An Economic Perspective on Maritime Predation' (1995), in C.R. Pennell (ed.), *Bandits at Sea: A Pirates Reader* (New York: New York University Press, 2001), p. 83.

8 Raphael Perl, *Trends in Terrorism: 2006*, RL33555, (Washington DC: Congressional Research Service, 2006), pp. 5–6, available at http://www.hls-watch.com/sitedocs/RL33555.pdf.

Chapter One

1 In *Re. Piracy Jure Gentium*, 1934 App. Cas 586, 598, reprinted in 3 Brit. int'l cases 836, 842 (1965) and cited in Malvina Halberstam, 'Terrorism on the High Seas: The *Achille Lauro*, Piracy and the IMO Convention on Maritime Safety', *The American Journal of International Law*, vol. 82, no. 2, April 1988, p. 273.

2 Anderson, 'Piracy and World History: An Economic Perspective on Maritime Predation', p. 82.

3 ICC International Maritime Bureau, *Piracy and Armed Robbery Against Ships: Annual Report 2006* (Barking: ICC Publishing, 2006) (covering period 1 January–31 December 2005), p. 3 [hereafter all such reports will be referred to using 'ICC Piracy Report, year' formula].

4 Available at http://www.un.org/Depts/los/convention_agreements/texts/unclos/unclos_e.pdf, p. 61.

5 See for example Vijay Sakhuja, 'Maritime Order and Piracy', *Strategic Analysis*, vol. 23, no. 5, August 2000, pp. 923–38; Sam Bateman, 'Maritime Transnational Violence – Problems of Control and Jurisdiction', paper for seminar on 'Transnational Crime', APCSS Biennial Conference, Honolulu, 16–18 July 2002; Peter Chalk, *Grey-Area Phenomena in Southeast Asia: Piracy, Drug Trafficking and Political Terrorism* (Canberra: Strategic and Defence Studies Centre, The Australian National University 1997), p. 37.

6 House of Commons Transport Committee, *Piracy*, HC 1026 (London: The Stationery Office, 2006), p. 11.

7 John S. Burnett, *Dangerous Waters: Modern Piracy and Terror on the High Seas* (New York: Dutton, 2002), p. 117. He notes that the increase in Malacca Strait and South China Sea piracy coincided with the Asian financial crisis of the 1990s.

8 Anderson, 'Piracy and World History: An Economic Perspective on Maritime Predation', p. 84; OECD Maritime Transport Committee, *Security in Maritime Transport: Risk Factors and Economic Impact*, (Paris: OECD, July 2003), p. 13.

9 For a review of these difficulties see Martin N. Murphy, 'Piracy and UNCLOS: Does International Law Help Regional States Combat Piracy?' in Lehr (ed.), *Violence at Sea: Piracy in the Age of Terrorism*, pp. 155–82.

10 For a full discussion of SUA and the thinking behind it, see Tullio Treves in Natalino Ronzitti (ed.), *Maritime Terrorism and International Law* (Dordrecht, Boston, MA and London: Martinus Nijhoff Publishers, 1990), pp. 69–90.

11 See Robert C. Beckman, 'Combatting Piracy and Armed Robbery Against Ships in Southeast Asia: The Way Forward', *Ocean Development and International Law*, vol. 33, nos 3–4, July 2002, pp. 321–2 and 329.

12 Jack A. Gottschalk and Brian P. Flanagan, *Jolly Roger with an Uzi: The Rise and Threat of Modern Piracy* (Annapolis, MD: Naval Institute Press, 2000), p. 3.

13 Barbara Conway, *The Piracy Business* (London: Hamlyn, 1981), p. 15.

14 The first recorded piracy incident off Somalia took place on 12 January 1991. The MV *Naviluck* was attacked by three boatloads of pirates off Xaafuun in the north. Three of the crew were taken ashore and killed. The remainder were forced overboard and were later rescued by a trawler. US Office of Naval Intelligence (ONI), *Worldwide Threats to Shipping Report*, ref. no. 1991–94, 12 January 1991. Although this was the first piracy report as such, the waters off Somalia were lawless before 1991.

15 On Indonesia, see for example the comments of Eric Frécon in Richel Langit-Dursin, 'Indonesia Key to End Piracy in Malacca Straits', *The Jakarta Post*, 6 August 2006.

16 See Thomas B. Hunter, 'The Growing Threat of Modern Piracy', US Naval

Institute *Proceedings,* vol. 125, no. 7, July 1999, p. 75.

17 Chalk, in 'Threats to the Maritime Environment: Piracy and Terrorism', paper presented to RAND Stakeholder Consultation, 28–30 October 2002. Also interview with Chalk, August 2004.

18 A point confirmed by IMB director Pottengal Mukundan. Interview, London, April 2004.

19 This is the case in a number of countries: on China see for example Nayan Chanda, 'Foot in the Water', *Far Eastern Economic Review,* 9 March 2000; Jon Vagg, 'Rough Seas? Contemporary Piracy in South East Asia', *British Journal of Criminology,* vol. 35, no. 1, Winter 1995, pp. 63–80; on Indonesia see for example Michael Richardson, 'Crackdown on Piracy', *Asia–Pacific Defence Reporter,* October–November 1992; and on military involvement in particular, Tim Huxley, *Disintegrating Indonesia? Implications for Regional Security,* Adelphi Paper 349 (Oxford: Oxford University Press for the IISS, 2002), p. 82; on West Africa see Gottschalk and Flanagan, *Jolly Roger with an Uzi: The Rise and Threat of Modern Piracy,* p. 64.

20 See Bruce Grant, *The Boat People: An Age Investigation* (Harmondsworth: Penguin, 1979); and Nghia M. Vo, *The Vietnamese Boat People, 1954 and 1975–1992* (Jefferson, NC and London: McFarland & Co., 2006).

21 Marcus Hand, 'Indonesian Soldier Arrested for Piracy', *Lloyd's List,* 4 January 2006.

22 Langit-Dursin, 'Indonesia Key to End Piracy in Malacca Straits'.

23 See http://www.cargosecurityinternational. com/channeldetail.asp?cid=4&caid=6619 for details.

24 E.D. Dickinson, 'Is the Crime of Piracy Obsolete?', *Harvard Law Review,* vol. 38, 1924–5, pp. 334–60. Also James Cable, *Gunboat Diplomacy 1919–1991,* third edition (New York: St Martin's Press, 1994), pp. 152–3. A.W. Grazebrook points out that patrolling against piracy

was the primary role of Britain's China Station right up until World War II: A.W. Grazebrook, 'Naval Forces and the Control of Piracy in Southeast Asia', *Naval Forces,* vol. 6, no. 1, 1995, p. 58.

25 For a description of Riau-Lingga piracy see Vagg, 'Rough Seas? Contemporary Piracy in South East Asia', pp. 69–74. See also Pyeatt Menefee, *Trends in Maritime Violence,* p. 132 on the existence of 'pirate societies' in Southeast Asia, the Red Sea and – arguably – the Caribbean; the social acceptability of piracy in Southeast Asia has been noted by several writers including Vagg; see 'Rough Seas? Contemporary Piracy in South East Asia', pp. 67–8; I.R. Hyslop, 'Contemporary Piracy', in Eric Ellen (ed.), *Piracy at Sea* (Paris: ICC Publishing, 1989), pp. 12 and 28, and Michael Pugh, 'Is Mahan Still Alive? State Naval Power in the International System', *Journal of Conflict Studies,* vol. 17, no. 2, Fall 1996, p. 2.

26 OECD Maritime Transport Committee, *Security in Maritime Transport: Risk Factors and Economic Impact,* p. 14.

27 Vagg, 'Rough Seas? Contemporary Piracy in South East Asia', pp. 73–4.

28 Stefan Eklöf, *Pirates in Paradise* (Copenhagen: NIAS Press, 2006), pp. 100–1.

29 Interview with IMB director Pottengal Mukundan, London, 2005; Eklöf, 'Piracy: Real Menace or Red Herring?', Asia Times Online, 4 August 2005, available at http://www.atimes.com/atimes/ Southeast_Asia/GH04Ae01.html.

30 Interview with Peter Chalk, London, August 2004. Mark J. Valencia, 'Piracy and Terrorism in Southeast Asia: Similarities, Differences and their Implications', in Derek Johnson and Mark Valencia (eds), *Piracy in Southeast Asia: Status, Issues and Responsibilities* (Singapore: ISEAS Publications, 2005), p. 80.

31 Sam Bateman, Catherine Zara Raymond and Joshua Ho, 'Safety and Security in the Malacca and Singapore Straits',

Institute of Defence and Strategic Studies policy paper (Singapore: Institute of Defence and Strategic Studies, May 2006), p. 22, available at http://www.idss.edu.sg/publications/conference_reports/IDSS%20S&S%20book.pdf.

[32] The House of Commons Transport Committee refers to the UK Department for Transport's Maritime Accident Investigation Branch 2004 annual report, which points to fatigue rates at 'elevated levels' and poor working practices that are 'classic symptoms of fatigue'. House of Commons Transport Committee, *Piracy*, p. 21.

[33] Bateman *et al.*, 'Safety and Security in the Malacca and Singapore Straits', p. 22; Thomas Turner, 'Bulk Carriers "Top of Pirate Hit List"', *Lloyd's List*, 9 May 2006.

[34] Bateman *et al.*, *ibid.*, p. 21.

[35] Bateman *et al.*, *ibid.*, p. 22.

[36] Mark C. Farley, 'International and Regional Trends in Maritime Policy, 1989–1993', masters thesis, Naval Postgraduate School, 1993, p. 23.

[37] For a useful overview of pirates' boarding methods, see Rupert Herbert-Burns, 'Compound Piracy at Sea in the Early Twenty-First Century: A Tactical to Operational-Level Perspective on Contemporary, Multiphase Piratical Methodology', in Lehr (ed.), *Violence at Sea: Piracy in the Age of Terrorism*, pp. 104–11.

[38] See Clarence Fernandez, 'World Body Opposes Weapons on Ships to Fight Piracy', Reuters AlertNet, 19 September 2006.

[39] 'No empirical work has been done on the cost of piracy, certainly in comparison with the cost of suppression.' Interview with Chalk, London, August 2004.

[40] Eric Ellis, 'Piracy on the High Seas is on the Rise in South-East Asia', *Fortune*, 29 September 2003, available at http://www.singapore-window.org/sw03/030919fo.htm.

[41] Chalk, 'Maritime Piracy: A Global Overview', *Jane's Intelligence Review*, vol. 12, no. 8, August 2000, p. 50.

[42] Burnett, *Dangerous Waters: Modern Piracy and Terror on the High Seas*, p. 70.

[43] Sakhuja, 'Sea Piracy: India Boosts Countermeasures', Institute of Peace and Conflict Studies Article No. 987, 14 March 2003.

[44] OECD Maritime Transport Committee, *Security in Maritime Transport: Risk Factors and Economic Impact*, p. 10.

[45] As regards insurance, marine underwriters to date have, in the main, been able to treat piracy as a low- to medium-level nuisance. See Vivian Schlesinger, 'Piracy Not Hitting Insurance Rates', *Journal of Commerce Online*, 13 January 2003.

[46] This is based on a WTO estimate for world merchandise trade in 2005 of $10.5 trillion. The WTO's figure has been discounted by 25% to reflect the principle that 75% of the world's trade *by value* moves by sea (as compared to 90% by volume). See WTO, *International Trade Statistics 2006*, Table 1.3: 'Growth in the Value of World Merchandise Trade by Region 2005', p. 16, available at http://www.wto.org/english/res_e/statis_e/its2006_e/its06_overview_e.pdf.

[47] The $500bn estimate dates from 1993, and includes trade passing through the Lombok and Sundra Straits and passing by the Spratly Islands in the South China Sea. In 1995, world maritime trade was estimated to amount to $2tr. The $2tr figure for the Malacca Strait is extrapolated from previous estimates of the value of trade passing though the regional straits (of which the Malacca is by far the most significant), on the assumption of a steady growth rate. For the 1993 data, see John H. Noer with David Gregory, *Maritime Economic Interests and the Sea Lines of Communication Through the South China Sea: The Value of Trade in Southeast Asia* (Alexandria, VA: Center for Naval Analyses, 1996), p. 2.

[48] The figure of $5,000 per attack was suggested by the deputy director of the IMB, Jayant Abhyankar, and quoted in Gottschalk and Flanagan, *Jolly Roger with an Uzi: The Rise and Threat of Modern*

Piracy, p. 88. Calculation in Eklöf, *Pirates in Paradise*, p. 99.

49 Gottschalk and Flanagan, *Jolly Roger with an Uzi: The Rise and Threat of Modern Piracy*, pp. 93–4.

50 Dragonette, 'Lost at Sea', p. 174. By contrast, Dana R. Dillon argues that increased costs due to piracy can act as a non-tariff trade barrier. The costs of using the most dangerous ports can be sufficiently high to discourage ship-owners from taking cargo there, creating, in effect, a form of boycott: 'Piracy in Asia: A Growing Barrier to International Trade', The Heritage Foundation *Backgrounder*, no. 1379, 22 June 2000, p. 2.

51 Interview with IMB director Pottengal Mukundan, London, April 2004.

52 Conversation with Andrew Linnington, London, August 2006.

53 Chalk, *Non-Military Security and Global Order: The Impact of Extremism, Violence and Chaos on National and International Security* (London: Macmillan, 2000), p. 66. An example is that of the master and chief engineer of the *Alondra Rainbow*, hijacked in 1999 en route to Japan from Indonesia.

54 See http://www.icc-ccs.org/prc/piracy report.php.

55 See http://www.imo.org/home.asp.

56 See http://www.nga.mil/portal/site/ maritime/.

57 See IMO, 'Piracy and Armed Robbery at Sea', available at http://www.oceans atlas.com/unatlas/issues/safety/transport_ telecomm/maritime_sec/piracy2k.htm.

58 Bateman *et al.*, 'Safety and Security in the Malacca and Singapore Straits', p. 23.

59 'Indonesia – Pirates Have Better Equipment', *Fairplay*, 2 November 2006.

60 UK Defence Intelligence Staff figure from Defence Intelligence Analysis Staff, 'Maritime Piracy Today', classified, Ministry of Defence, 10 July 1998, p. 1; Australian Defence Intelligence Organisation figure from Defence Intelligence Organisation, 'Maritime Piracy: Rough Seas Ahead?', classified, Department of Defence, October 1996, p.

3, both quoted in *Threats and Challenges to Maritime Security 2020*, prepared by ONI and US Coast Guard Intelligence Coordination Center, 1 March 1999, p. 16.

61 Nippon Foundation, *Survey on Acts of Piracy and Armed Robbery against Japanese Shipping Companies*, 1999, cited in House of Commons Transport Committee, *Piracy*, p. 12.

62 ICC Piracy Report, 2006, p. 16.

63 Bateman, 'Maritime Transnational Violence – Problems of Control and Jurisdiction', p. 4. In an interview in April 2004, IMB director Pottengal Mukundan observed that under-reporting was 'substantial'.

64 John Grissim, 'Pirates Again Stalking the Seven Seas', *The World Paper*, May 1997.

65 Chalk, *Grey-Area Phenomena in Southeast Asia: Piracy, Drug Trafficking and Political Terrorism*, pp. 28–9.

66 'Anti-Piracy Agreement Signed by 11 Asian Countries', *The Star Online*, 21 June 2006, available at http://thestar. com.my/news/story.asp?file=/2006/6/21/ nation/20060621151412&sec=nation; 'Factsheet on the Regional Cooperation Agreement on Combating Piracy and Armed Robbery Against Ships in Asia (ReCAAP)', undated, available at https://app-pac.mica.gov.sg/data/ vddp/embargo/21075516.pdf. For more information on ReCAAP, see 'Regional Agreement Against Maritime Piracy to Take Effect in September', People's Daily Online, 21 June 2006, available at http://english.people.com.cn/200606/21/ eng20060621_275965.html; Hand, 'Asian Alliance to Fight Piracy Goes Ahead Despite Dissenters', *Lloyd's List*, 22 June 2006; ONI, *Worldwide Threats to Shipping Report*, 5 July 2006.

67 ISC reports can be found at http://www. recaap.org/publish/recaap/reports.html.

68 See for example Donald Urquhart, 'Time to Close the Piracy Gap', *The Business Times*, 29 November 2006.

69 These figures can be found in the ICC Piracy Report, 2007.

[70] Quoted in Grant, *The Boat People: An Age Investigation*, p. 64.

[71] Interview with Bronson Percival, senior adviser on South East Asia, Centre for Naval Analyses, Washington DC, June 2006.

[72] Langit-Dursin, 'Indonesia Key to End Piracy in Malacca Straits'.

[73] The ONI comments, 'past reporting from officials states that pirate gangs operating off the coast were viewed as latter day Robin Hoods by some of the villages in the region'. ONI, *Worldwide Threats to Shipping Report*, 5 July 2006.

[74] Ed Davies, 'Indonesia Counts its Islands before it's Too Late', Reuters, 16 May 2007, available at http://uk.reuters.com/article/environmentNews/idUKJAK7973020070515.

[75] John F. Bradford, 'Japanese Anti-Piracy Initiatives in Southeast Asia: Policy Formulations and the Coastal State Responses', *Contemporary Southeast Asia*, vol. 26, no. 3, 2004, pp. 497–9. The fact that, according to the IMB, only 1% of the traffic transiting the Malacca Strait actually trades with Indonesia could influence the country's attitude to Malacca Strait security. Figure cited in House of Commons Transport Committee, *Piracy*, Evidence (Ev.) 28.

[76] Eklöf, 'Piracy: A Critical Perspective', *International Institute for Asian Studies Newsletter*, no. 36, March 2005.

[77] On under-reporting, see Chalk, *Grey-Area Phenomena in Southeast Asia: Piracy, Drug Trafficking and Political Terrorism*, p. 29. On the Philippine navy and coast guard estimates, see Eduardo Ma. R. Santos, 'Piracy and Armed Robbery against Ships in the Philippines', in Graham Gerald Ong-Webb (ed.), *Piracy, Maritime Terrorism and Securing the Malacca Straits* (Singapore: Institute of Southeast Asian Studies, 2006), pp. 39–40.

[78] See Edith Regalado, 'NSA: RP Can't Police Sea Lanes Between Mindanao, Indonesia', *The Philippine Star*, 16 October 2006.

[79] 'Indonesia Identifies Three Groups in Sea Crimes', Channel News Asia, 31 May 2005, available at http://www.channelnewsasia.com/stories/southeastasia/print/150342/1/.html.

[80] Eklöf, 'Piracy: Real Menace or Red Herring?'.

[81] Bateman *et al.*, 'Safety and Security in the Malacca and Singapore Straits', p. 20.

[82] Burnett, *Dangerous Waters: Modern Piracy and Terror on the High Seas*, pp. 134–45.

[83] S. Ramesh, '"Eyes in the Sky" Initiative Launched for Malacca Strait Security', Channel News Asia, 13 September 2005, available at http://www.channelnewsasia.com/stories/singaporelocalnews/view/168037/1/.html; see also http://www.iiss.org/whats-new/iiss-in-the-press/press-coverage-2005/september-2005/sky-eye-opens-asean-nations-join-forces.

[84] See Stefano Ambrogi, 'Pirate Attacks on the Wane', Reuters, 7 May 2005, reporting a note of caution sounded by the IMB.

[85] On 2006 incidents, see 'Pirate Attacks in Malacca Strait', BBC News, 4 July 2006, available at http://news.bbc.co.uk/1/hi/world/asia-pacific/5143858.stm?ls. On the wider implications of these attacks, see Urquhart, 'New Malacca Pirate Attacks Raise Concern', *Business Times*, 5 July 2006.

[86] For a thorough review of the continuing pirate predation on Malaysian fishermen, see J.N. Mak, 'Pirates, Renegades and Fishermen: The Politics of "Sustainable" Piracy in the Strait of Malacca' in Lehr (ed.), *Violence at Sea: Piracy in the Age of Terrorism*, pp. 199–223.

[87] Sakhuja, 'Indian Ocean and the Safety of Sea Lines of Communication', *Strategic Analysis*, vol. 25, no. 5, August 2001.

[88] Simon Montlake, 'Hard Times for Pirates in Busy World Waterway', *Christian Science Monitor*, 30 October 2006, available at http://www.csmonitor.com/2006/1030/p01s04-woap.html.

[89] IMO Maritime Safety Committee Circular 698 (MSC/Circ. 698), 30 June 1995, p. 3.

[90] Chalk, 'Maritime Piracy: A Global Overview', p. 75.

91 For more detail on African piracy, see Chalk, 'Africa Suffers Wave of Maritime Violence', RAND Commentary, 2001, available at http://www.rand.org/commentary/040101JIR.html.

92 There are many accounts of the attack on the *Seabourn Spirit*. For a basic account, see 'Cruise Ship Repels Somali Pirates', BBC News, 5 November 2005, available at http://news.bbc.co.uk/1/hi/world/africa/4409662.stm. Speculation that it had been mounted by terrorists followed the attack: 'Missile "Embedded in US Cruise Ship"', WorldNetDaily, 7 November 2005, available at http://www.worldnetdaily.com/news/article.asp?ARTICLE_ID=47257.

93 See 'Somalia: Security Council Urges Action Over Piracy Off the Coast of Somalia in Line With IMO Assembly Resolution', *Cargo Security International*, 17 March 2006, available at http://www.cargosecurityinternational.com/channeldetail.asp?cid=4&caid=6619;also Richard Meade, 'Cruise Attack Sparks UN Action', *Fairplay*, 10 November 2005.

94 For background on the ICU, see Michael A. Weinstein, 'The Islamic Courts Union Opens a New Chapter In Somalia's Political History', *Power and Interest News Report (PINR)*, 19 June 2006, available at http://www.pinr.com/report.php?ac=view_printable&report_id=512&language_id=1.

95 ONI, *Worldwide Threats to Shipping Report*, 20 December 2006.

96 Aweys Osman Yusuf, 'Somali Pirates Gather at the Coastal Town of Haradhdere', Shabelle Media Network, 26 January 2007, available at http://www.shabelle.net/news/ne2172.htm; 'Pirates Hijack UN Food Aid Ship', Associated Press, 25 February 2007, available at http://www.thestar.com/printArticle/185547; Mohamed Amiin, 'Pirates Seize Commercial Vessel off Somali Coast', Shabelle Media Network, 2 April 2007, available at http://www.shabelle.net/news/ne2669.htm.

97 ONI Worldwide Threats to Shipping Special Advisory, 17 May 2007; Hand, 'Somalia Pirates Using "Mother Vessel" Tactics', *Lloyd's List*, 18 May 2007.

98 It is worth taking note of the press release issued by Andrew Mwangura of the Seafarers' Assistance Programme, Mombasa, Kenya, on 8 February 2006, available at http://www.ecop.info/english/e-sap-net-39.htm.

99 'Somalia's Dangerous Waters', BBC News, 26 September 2005, available at http://news.bbc.co.uk/1/hi/world/africa/4283396.stm; see also US Department of Transportation, Maritime Administration (MARAD), MARAD Advisory 05-03, 28 October 2005, which advises ships to keep at a distance of 200nm from the coast. Available at http://www.marad.dot.gov/headlines/advisories/ADV_0503.htm.

100 Hand, 'Somali Pirates Move Even Further from the Coast', *Lloyd's List*, 14 November 2005; interview with IMB Director Pottengal Mukundan, 2005.

101 Scott Coffen-Smout, undated, 'Pirates, Warlords and Rogue Fishing Vessels in Somalia's Unruly Seas', available at http://www.chebucto.ns.ca/~ar120/somalia.html; also 'US Captures 13 Somali "Pirates"', BBC News, 19 March 2006, available at http://news.bbc.co.uk/1/hi/world/africa/4822722.stm.

102 Abdulkadir Khalif, 'How Illegal Fishing Feeds Somali Piracy', *The East African* (Nairobi), 15 November 2005.

103 On the *Dongwon-ho*, see Bo-Mi Lim, 'Militants Who Seize S. Korea Ship Off Somalia Say They're Defending Against Illegal Fishing', NC Times.com, 5 April 2006, available at http://www.nctimes.com/articles/2006/04/06/news/nation/16_12_004_5_06.txt.

104 'Extracts from the Report of the IMO Working Group on the Malacca Strait Area', annexe to IMO, *Piracy And Armed Robbery Against Ships: Recommendations to Governments for Combating Piracy and Armed Robbery Against Ships*, Maritime Safety Committee

Circular 622 (MSC/Circ. 622), 22 June 1993.

[105] Anderson, 'Piracy and World History: An Economic Perspective on Maritime Predation', pp. 86 and 93–4.

[106] *Ibid.,* p. 98.

[107] Chalk, 'Threats to the Maritime Environment: Piracy and Terrorism', p. 7.

[108] Alex Perry, 'Buccaneer Tales in the Pirates' Lair', 2001, TIMEAsia.com, available at http://www.time.com/time/asia/features/journey2001/pirates.html, provides a detailed description of a hijacking involving a sleeper.

[109] See ICC Piracy Report, 2003, p. 24.

[110] For a history of this form of piracy, see Abhyankar, 'Maritime Fraud and Piracy', pp. 187–91.

[111] ISC *Report for December 2006*, p. 10, available at http://www.recaap.org/publish/etc/medialib/recaap_public_reports.Par.5428.File.dat/ISC%20Report%20for%20December%202006.pdf. NB: this incident was not reported to the IMB.

[112] Pyeatt Menefee, *Trends in Maritime Violence*, p. 126; Conway, *The Piracy Business*, p. 20; OECD Maritime Transport Committee, *Security in Maritime Transport: Risk Factors and Economic Impact*, p. 14.

[113] For more detail on the phantom ship phenomenon and how it evolved out of hull and cargo frauds, see Abhyankar, 'Maritime Fraud and Piracy', pp. 175–83.

[114] Pyeatt Menefee, *Trends in Maritime Violence*, pp. 126–7; Conway, *The Piracy Business*, pp. 15–17.

[115] On the *Doo Yang Jade*, see Mukundan, 'Cargo Frauds', presentation to the International Union of Marine Insurance Annual Conference, London, 10–14 September 2000.

[116] Abhyankar, 'Maritime Fraud and Piracy', *Transnational Organised Crime*, vol. 4, no. 3–4, Autumn–Winter 1998, p. 180.

[117] On the increasing lawlessness in Nigeria see International Crisis Group, 'Nigeria: Failed Elections, Failing State?', *Africa Report No. 126*, 30 May 2007, pp. 9–11, available at http://www.crisisgroup.org/library/documents/africa/west_africa/126_nigeria_failed_elections.pdf.

[118] Anthony Davis, 'Piracy in Southeast Asia Shows Signs of Increased Organisation', *Jane's Intelligence Review*, vol. 16, no. 6, June 2004, pp. 38 and 39. On crew members being killed, see Hand, 'Piracy Attacks Leave Owners Facing Ransom Cover Dilemma', *Lloyd's List*, 24 June 2005.

[119] See 'Pirates Free Indonesian Hostages', BBC News, 19 March 2005, available at http://news.bbc.co.uk/1/hi/world/asia-pacific/4363741.stm. Also Bateman *et al.*, 'Safety and Security in the Malacca and Singapore Straits', p. 21.

[120] Kate McGeown, 'Aceh Rebels Blamed for Piracy', BBC News, 8 September 2003, available at http://news.bbc.co.uk/1/hi/world/asia-pacific/3090136.stm; Catherine Zara Raymond, 'Piracy in Southeast Asia: New Trends, Issues and Responses', *Harvard Asia Quarterly*, vol. 9, no. 4, Fall 2005, available at http://www.asiaquarterly.com/index.php?option=com_content&task=view&id=30&Itemid=1.

[121] Chalk, 'Maritime Piracy: A Global Overview', p. 47; Jack Hitt, 'Bandits in the Global Shipping Lanes', *The New York Times Magazine*, 20 August 2000.

[122] Davis, 'Piracy in Southeast Asia Shows Signs of Increased Organisation', p. 37.

[123] Pino Arlacchi, 'The Dynamics of Illegal Markets', in Phil Williams and Dimitri Vlassis (eds), *Combating Transnational Crime: Concepts, Actvities and Responses* (Abingdon & New York: Frank Cass, 2001), pp. 7–8.

[124] 'Dead Men Tell No Tales', *The Economist*, 16 December 1999. Also Tom McCawley, 'Sea of Trouble', *Far East Economic Review*, 27 May 2004.

[125] Chalk, 'Maritime Piracy: A Global Overview', pp. 49–50. See also Neil Renwick and Jason Abbott, 'Piratical Violence and Maritime Security in South East Asia', *Security Dialogue*, vol. 30, no. 2, June 1999, pp. 186–7.

126 On the steps China is taking to improve maritime security see Zhang Shouguo, 'China – Playing an Active Role in Fulfilling Maritime Security Obligations', paper presented to OECD Workshop on Maritime Transport, Paris, 4–5 November 2004, available at http://www.oecd.org/dataoecd/19/61/33949707.pdf. However, its drive for international respectability has not stopped the country being a destination for stolen raw materials. See Malcolm Moore, 'Record Copper Prices Power China's Black Market Demand for Hot Metal', *Daily Telegraph,* 16 June 2006, available at http://www.telegraph.co.uk/money/main.jhtml?xml=/money/2006/06/17/cncopp17.xml.

127 Abhyankar, 'Maritime Fraud and Piracy', p. 180.

128 Jane MacCartney, 'Asian Piracy Costs $25 Bn a Year, Says Expert', Reuters, 11 December 2002, available at http://www.planetark.com/avantgo/dailynewsstory.cfm?newsid=18987.

129 Dragonette, 'Lost at Sea', p. 174.

130 Peter Earle, *The Pirate Wars* (London: Methuen, 2003), pp. 20–21.

131 See http://www.icgg.org/corruption.cpi_2006_data.html.

132 On 'Captain Changco', see Michael S. McDaniel, 'Modern High Seas Piracy', presentation to the Propeller Club of the United States, 20 November 2000, available at http://www.cargolaw.com/presentations_pirates.html. On Chew Cheng Kiat, see Robert Stuart, *In Search of Pirates: A Modern Day Odyssey in the South China Sea* (Edinburgh: Mainstream Publishing, 2002), p. 139.

133 Anderson, 'Piracy and World History: An Economic Perspective on Maritime Predation', p. 84.

134 Max G. Manwaring, *Street Gangs: The New Urban Insurgency* (Carlisle, PA: US Army War College, Strategic Studies Institute, 2005), pp. 7 and 12–15; Mark Stevenson, 'Mexico: Drug Gangs Using Terror Tactics', Associated Press, 18 May 2007, available at http://www.guardian.co.uk/worldlatest/story/0,,-6642334,00.html.

135 Chalk, 'Maritime Piracy: A Global Overview', p. 50.

Chapter Two

1 Since the 1960s there have been fewer than 200 maritime terrorist incidents, compared with over 10,000 terrorist incidents in total. 'Piracy and Terrorism Should Not Be Conflated', *Jane's Intelligence Review,* vol. 16, no. 8, August 2004, p. 57.

2 Chalk, 'Maritime Terrorism in the Contemporary Era: Threat and Potential Future Contingencies', in *The MIPT Terrorism Annual 2006* (Oklahoma City, OK: National Memorial Institute for the Prevention of Terrorism, 2006) p. 21.

3 On the hijack as a military success but a political failure for the US, see Charles T. Eppright, '"Counterterrorism" and Conventional Military Force: The Relationship between Political Effect and Utility', *Studies in Conflict and Terrorism,* vol. 20, no. 4, 1997, p. 341.

4 See Daniel Benjamin and Steven Simon, *The Age of Sacred Terror* (New York: Random House, 2003), pp. 323–4; Richard A. Clarke, *Against All Enemies: Inside America's War on Terror* (London: Free Press, 2004), pp. 222–3, particularly on the failures of inter-service communication that allowed the ship to be exposed to unnecessary risk; and Harold W. Gehman Jr, 'Lost Patrol: The Attack on the USS *Cole*', US Naval Institute *Proceedings*, vol. 127, no. 4, April 2001, pp. 34–7 on the inquiry that followed the attack and preventive measures to be taken in the future.

5 See Simon Elegant, 'The Return of Abu Sayyaf', *TIME Asia,* 23 August 2004,

available at http://www.time.com/time/
asia/magazine/article/0,13673,50104083
0-686107,00.html; Rommel C. Banlaoi,
'Maritime Terrorism in Southeast Asia:
The Abu Sayyaf Threat', *Naval War
College Review,* Winter 2005, pp. 71–2;
Zachary Abuza, *Balik Terrorism: The
Return of the Abu Sayyaf* (Carlisle, PA:
Strategic Studies Institute, US Army War
College, September 2005), p. 1, available
at http://www.strategicstudiesinstitute.
army.mil/pdffiles/PUB625.pdf; and p. 10,
where he refers to signs that the group
was planning a further round of attacks
on *SuperFerries* in 2004.

6   Davis, 'Tamil Tigers Seek to Rebuild
Naval Force', *Jane's Intelligence Review,*
March 2005; R.S. Vasan, 'Sea Control and
the LTTE', *Strategic Trends,* vol. 4, no. 27,
Observer Research Foundation, 7 August
2006.

7   Banlaoi, 'Maritime Terrorism in
Southeast Asia: The Abu Sayyaf Threat',
p. 71.

8   V. Suryanarayan, 'Sea Tigers – Threat
to Indian Security', *The Hindu,*
28 July 2004, available at http://
www.thehindu.com/2004/07/28/
stories/2004072802311000.htm; Sakhuja,
'The Dynamics of LTTE's Commercial
Maritime Infrastructure', Observer
Research Foundation Occasional
Paper (New Delhi: Observer Research
Foundation, April 2006), p. 7.

9   Suryanarayan, 'Sea Tigers – Threat to
Indian Security'.

10 Sakhuja, 'The Dynamics of LTTE's
Commercial Maritime Infrastructure', p.
7.

11 For a brief biography of al-Nashiri, see
http://en.wikipedia.org/wiki/Abd_al-
Rahim_al-Nashiri. On his role within
al-Qaeda, see National Commission
on Terrorist Attacks Upon the United
States, *The 9/11 Commission Report,* 22
July 2004, pp. 152–3, available at http://
www.9-11commission.gov/report/
911Report.pdf; see also 'Suspected
Qaeda Chief Cooperating', CBS News, 22
November 2002, available at http://www.

cbsnews.com/stories/2002/11/17/attack/
main529656.shtml. It should be noted that
in his statement to the Combatant Status
Review Tribunal held at Guantanamo
Bay on 14 March 2007, al-Nashiri denied
all accusations made against him and
claimed his admissions had been made
under torture. A transcript of the statement
is available at http://www.defenselink.
mil/news/transcript_ISN10015.pdf.

12 Chalk, 'Maritime Terrorism in the
Contemporary Era: Threat and Potential
Future Contingencies', p. 35.

13 Pyeatt Menefee, *Trends in Maritime
Violence,* p. 97.

14 National Commission on Terrorist
Attacks upon the Unites States, *The
9/11 Commission Report*: on Khalid
Sheikh Mohammed, see pp. 145–50; on
al-Nashiri, pp. 152–3; on al-Nashiri's
reported confessions and plans, see
Michael Richardson, *A Time Bomb for
Global Trade: Maritime-Related Terrorism
in an Age of Weapons of Mass Destruction,*
(Singapore: Institute of Southeast Asian
Studies, 2004), pp. 18–20.

15 For discussion of terrorists' tactical
conservatism see for example Bruce
Hoffman, *Inside Terrorism* (London:
Gollancz, 1998), p. 198; and Grant
Wardlaw, *Political Terrorism: Theory,
Tactics and Counter-Measures* [1982],
second edition (Cambridge: Cambridge
University Press, 1989), p. 192; also Paul
Wilkinson, 'Technology and Terrorism',
Terrorism and Political Violence, vol. 5, no.
2, Summer 1993, pp. 4–5 who, whilst
agreeing that terrorists are tactically con-
servative, shows that they are prepared
to embrace technical innovation.

16 James Pelkofski, 'Before the Storm: Al-
Qaeda's Coming Maritime Campaign',
US Naval Institute *Proceedings,* vol.
131, no. 12, December 2005, p. 22; also
Chalk, 'Maritime Terrorism in the
Contemporary Era: Threat and Potential
Future Contingencies', p. 28.

17 On the move from 'spectacular' attacks
to less ambitious ones, see for example
Brian Michael Jenkins and Gregory

F. Treverton, 'Misjudging the Jihad: Briefing Osama on All the War's Wins and Losses', *San Francisco Chronicle*, 13 November 2005, available at http://www.sfgate.com/cgi-bin/article.cgi?f=/c/a/2005/11/13/INGUPFLGKH1.DTL&hw=brian+michael+jenkins&sn=003&sc=917; Perl, *Trends in Terrorism: 2006*.

18 'Group Claims Attack: Double Suicide Bombings', Associated Press, 25 April 2007, available at http://www.suburbanchicagonews.com/heraldnews/news/356058,4_1_JO25_IRAQ_S1.article.

19 Scott C. Truver, 'Mines, Improvised Explosives: A Threat to Global Commerce?', *National Defense*, April 2007, available at http://www.nationaldefensemagazine.org/issues/2007/April/Minesimprovided.htm.

20 On Jemaah Islamiah's connections with al-Qaeda, see Dan Murphy, 'Southeast Asia Easy Source of Al-Qaeda Recruits', *Christian Science Monitor*, 9 October 2002, available at http://www.csmonitor.com/2002/1009/p07s01-woap.html.

21 Peter Apps, 'Sri Lanka, Tigers Claim Victory in Naval Clash', Reuters AlertNet, 17 June 2006.

22 Martin N. Murphy, 'Maritime Threat: Tactics and Technology of the Sea Tigers', *Jane's Intelligence Review*, vol. 18, no. 6, June 2006, p. 9.

23 On al-Qaeda's interest, see John Mintz, '15 Freighters Believed to be Linked to Al-Qaeda', *The Washington Post*, 31 December 2002.

24 On the various criminal uses of submersibles and semi-submersibles, see Joshua Sinai, 'Future Trends in Worldwide Maritime Terrorism', *The Quarterly Journal*, vol. 3, no. 1, March 2004, p. 53.

25 'Drug Submarine Found in Colombia', BBC News, 7 September 2000, available at http://news.bbc.co.uk/1/hi/world/americas/915059.stm.

26 'Submarine Carrying 3 Tons of Cocaine Seized Off Costa Rica', *USA Today*, 21 November 2006, available at http://www.usatoday.com/news/world/2006-11-20-drug-submarine_x.htm?csp=34.

27 Sakhuja, 'Mini Submarine – A Vessel of Choice with Drug Cartels and Terrorists', South Asia Analysis Group, Paper No. 1313, 30 March 2005, available at http://www.saag.org/papers14/paper1312.html.

28 See Davis, 'Tracking Tigers in Phuket: A Secret Tamil Guerrilla Base Embarrasses Bangkok', Asiaweek.com, vol. 29, no. 23, 16 June 2000, available at http://www.asiaweek.com/asiaweek/magazine/2000/0616/nat.security.html; and Sakhuja, 'Mini Submarine – A Vessel of Choice with Drug Cartels and Terrorists'. Rohan Gunaratna also reports that the Sea Tigers attempted to build a submarine in India but their efforts there were also disrupted: Gunaratna, 'The Asymmetric Threat from Maritime Terrorism', *Jane's Navy International*, October 2001, pp. 26 and 28.

29 Sakhuja, 'Mini Submarine – A Vessel of Choice with Drug Cartels and Terrorists'.

30 Gunaratna, 'The Asymmetric Threat from Maritime Terrorism', p. 14. However, a website about the war in Sri Lanka claims that the Tigers have a midget submarine in their inventory; 'LTTE's Military Capability', undated although no later than 2005, http://www.tamiltigers.net.

31 'LTTE Might Be Trying to Acquire Submarine: Report', Zee News, 30 March 2007, available at http://www.zeenews.com/articles.asp?rep=2&aid=362824&sid=SAS&ssid.

32 See Mark Mazzetti and Thom Shanker, 'Hizbollah's Unexpected Firepower', *International Herald Tribune*, 19 July 2006, available at http://www.iht.com/articles/2006/07/19/news/missile.php; 'Hizbollah Brings Out Iranian Silkworm to Hit Israel Corvette', *DEBKAfile*, 15 July 2006, available at http://www.debka.com/article.php?aid=1184.

33 ONI, *Worldwide Threats to Shipping Report*, 26 July 2006; 'INS *Hanit* Suffers Iranian Missile Attack', Defense Update: News Analysis by David Eshel, 17 July 2006, available at http://www.defense-update.

com/2006/07/ins-hanit-suffers-iranian-missile.html.

34 Harry de Quetteville, 'Terrorists' Missiles Are From Teheran Armoury', *Daily Telegraph*, 17 July 2006, available at http://www.telegraph.co.uk/news/main.jhtml?xml=/news/2006/07/17/wmid317.xml; Toby Harnden, 'Iran Admits It Gave Hizbollah Missiles to Hit All Israel', *Sunday Telegraph*, 6 August 2006, available at http://www.telegraph.co.uk/news/main.jhtml?xml=/news/2006/08/06/wmid206.xml.

35 Memorial Institute for the Prevention of Terrorism, 'Popular Forces of April 25 Attacked Military Target, 28 January 1985, Portugal', Terrorism Knowledge Base Incident Profile, available at http://www.tkb.org/Incident.jsp?incID=4049.

36 Tim Butcher, 'Missile Attack on US Ship in Jordanian Red Sea Port', *Daily Telegraph*, 20 August 2005, available at http://www.telegraph.co.uk/news/main.jhtml?xml=/news/2005/08/20/wjordan20.xml.

37 For a report on this plot, see Julian Borger, 'Plot to Sink Warship on 9/11', *Guardian*, 21 February 2003, available at http://www.guardian.co.uk/alqaida/story/0,,900071,00.html.

38 'Bin Laden: Goal is to Bankrupt the US', CNN.com, 1 November 2004, available at http://www.cnn.com/2004/WORLD/meast/11/01/binladen.tape/.

39 Martin N. Murphy, 'Slow Alarm: The Response of the Marine Insurance Industry to the Threat of Piracy and Maritime Terrorism', *Maritime Studies*, no. 148, May–June 2006, p. 4; Richardson, *A Time Bomb for Global Trade: Maritime-Related Terrorism in an Age of Weapons of Mass Destruction*, pp. 70–1.

40 Adam Porter, 'Global Refinery Shortage Shifts Power Balance', BBC News, 2 October 2005, available at http://news.bbc.co.uk/1/hi/business/4296812.stm.

41 See 'Blasts Target Iraqi Oil Terminals', BBC News, 25 April 2004, available at http://news.bbc.co.uk/1/hi/world/middle_east/3656481.stm; John C.K.

Daly, 'The Threat to Iraqi Oil', the Jamestown Foundation *Terrorism Monitor*, vol. 2, no. 12, 17 June 2004, available at http://www.jamestown.org/publications_details.php?volume_id=400&issue_id=2990&article_id=2368122. On the continuing need to protect these terminals, see Jim Garamone, '"Ring of Steel" Encircles Iraqi Oil Platforms', American Forces Press Service, 15 July 2006, available at http://www.defenselink.mil/news/May2006/20060501_4986.html.

42 The US navy, however, has an 'absolute concern' that al-Qaeda will mount further attacks at sea, against oil targets in particular. See Ambrogi, 'US Navy Says Al-Qaeda Poses Major Threat From Sea', Reuters AlertNet, 3 July 2006.

43 'Security Experts Say Cruise Ships a Soft Target', *Houston Chronicle*, 20 November 2001, available at http://www.chron.com/disp/story.mpl/special/terror/front/1139846.html. See also Chalk, 'Maritime Terrorism in the Contemporary Era: Threat and Potential Future Contingencies', pp. 26–7.

44 Murad Sezer, 'Terror Suspect: "I Was Going to Attack Israeli Ships"', *USA Today*, 11 August 2005, available at http://www.usatoday.com/news/world/2005-08-11-turkey-terror_x.htm.

45 Several cruise lines employ plain-clothes security staff, some of whom are ex-British Army Gurkhas, to confront terrorists. See Bill Glenton, 'A Sea Change Required on Security Risks', *Financial Times*, 7 September 2002.

46 See Don Walsh, 'Tourism and Terrorism: A Difficult Journey Ahead for the Cruise Ship Industry', *Sea Power*, December 2002, for a description of the risks confronting the industry, together with implemented and suggested counter-measures.

47 Martin N. Murphy, 'Slow Alarm: The Response of the Marine Insurance Industry to the Threat of Piracy and Maritime Terrorism', p. 20.

48 On the Halifax explosion, see Laura M. MacDonald, *Curse of the Narrows*

(New York: Walker & Company, 2005) pp. 60–73; Gottschalk and Flanagan, *Jolly Roger with an Uzi: The Rise and Threat of Modern Piracy*, p. 110; on Texas City, see http://en.wikipedia. org/wiki/Texas_City_disaster.

49   See Gottschalk and Flanagan, *Jolly Roger with an Uzi*, p. 110.

50   According to Michael Richardson, the ammonium nitrate aboard the *Grandcamp* had been manufactured originally as an explosive and subsequently altered. Richardson, *A Time Bomb for Global Trade: Maritime-Related Terrorism in an Age of Weapons of Mass Destruction*, p. 47.

51   'Toronto Bomb Plot: Ammonium Nitrate', *CBC News*, 5 June 2006, available at http://www.cbc.ca/news/background/toronto-bomb-plot/ammonium-nitrate.html.

52   OECD Maritime Transport Committee, *Security in Maritime Transport: Risk Factors and Economic Impact*, p. 12; Nic Fleming, 'The Cheap and Easy Recipe for Bombs', *Daily Telegraph*, 31 March 2004.

53   James A. Fay, 'Spills and Fires from LNG and Oil Tankers in Boston Harbour', 26 March 2003, available at http://www.wildcalifornia.org/cgi-files/0/pdfs/1076793808_Humboldt_Bay_LNG_Boston_Spills_Fay.pdf; Jerry Havens, 'Terrorism: Ready to Blow?', *Bulletin of the Atomic Scientists*, vol. 59, no. 4, 2003, pp. 16–18.

54   Interview with Gordon Milne, head of risk assessment, Lloyd's Register of Shipping, London, December 2005; Havens, 'Terrorism: Ready to Blow?'.

55   Interview with Milne; Havens, 'Terrorism: Ready to Blow?'; Paul Parfomak, 'Liquefied Natural Gas (LNG) Infrastructure Security: Background and Issues for Congress', Congressional Research Service, 16 March 2005, RL32073, available at http://ncseonline. org/nle/crsreports/05mar/RL32073.pdf, p. 9.

56   Interview with Milne.

57   Parfomak, 'Liquefied Natural Gas (LNG) Infrastructure Security: Background and Issues for Congress', p. 12; Ben Raines and Bill Finch, 'Holes in LNG Study', *Mobile Register*, 4 December 2003, available at http://www.borderpowerplants. org/pdf_docs/Holes_quest_study.pdf.

58   On the security arrangements, see Parfomak, 'Liquefied Natural Gas (LNG) Infrastructure Security: Background and Issues for Congress', pp. 13–19. See also Sandia National Laboratories, 'Guidance on Risk Analysis and Safety Implications of a Large Liquefied Natural Gas (LNG) Spill Over Water', SAND2004-6258, Sandia Report, December 2004, p. 15, available at http://www.energy.ca.gov/lng/documents/2004-12_SANDIA-DOE_RISK_ANALYSIS.PDF, p. 14. Shortly after 11 September 2001, the United States Coast Guard prevented an LNG ship from entering Boston harbour; no reason was given other than a heightened security risk: see 'LNG *Matthew* Banned from Boston', MarineLog.com, 27 September 2001. The publication of the Sandia Report has not dissuaded port authorities and many opinion formers, particularly those who might be affected by the construction of new LNG terminals, from being extremely nervous of LNG operations. Husick and Gale, for example, posit an unlikely scenario in which current port security precautions are circumvented: Lawrence A. Husick and Stephen Gale, 'Planning a Sea-borne Terrorist Attack', *Foreign Policy Research Institute*, 21 March 2005, available at http://www.fpri.org/enotes/20050321. americawar.husickgale.seaborneterrorist attack.html.

59   On the possibility of a tanker being run aground to cause oil pollution, see Luft and Korin, 'Terrorism Goes to Sea', p. 66. On the possibility of ships being used for environmental terrorism, see Chalk, 'Maritime Terrorism in the Contemporary Era: Threat and Potential Future Contingencies', p. 27. On environmental terrorism in general, see Elizabeth L. Chalecki, 'A New Vigilance: Identifying and Reducing the Risks

of Environmental Terrorism', Pacific Institute for Studies in Development, Environment, and Security Research Paper, September 2001, available at http://www.pacinst.org/reports/environment_and_terrorism/environ-mental_terrorism_final.pdf. On al-Qaeda's consideration of the use of oil tankers as weapons, see Peter Foster, 'Secret Arrest Yielded "Treasure Trove"', *Daily Telegraph*, 3 August 2004.

60 For detail on the cost of various terror attacks, see 'Al-Qaeda Operations Are Rather Cheap', *The Economist*, 10 April 2003, p. 45; Michael Buchanan, 'London Bombings Cost Just Hundreds', BBC News, 3 January 2006, available at http://news.bbc.co.uk/1/hi/uk/4576346.stm.

61 'Small Plane Crashes into Florida Building', BBC News, 6 January 2002, available at http://news.bbc.co.uk/1/hi/world/americas/1744923.stm; 'Plane Hits Milan Skyscraper', BBC News, 18 April 2002, available at http://news.bbc.co.uk/1/hi/world/europe/1937976.stm.

62 On the history of the container and its fundamental role in the globalisation phenomenon, see Marc Levinson, *The Box: How the Shipping Container Made the World Smaller and the World Economy Bigger* (Princeton, NJ: Princeton University Press, 2006).

63 See Robin M. Frost, *Nuclear Terrorism After 9/11*, Adelphi Paper 378 (Abingdon: Routledge for the IISS).

64 For a thorough examination of the issues, see Peter D. Zimmerman with Cheryl Loeb, 'Dirty Bombs: The Threat Revisited', *Defence Horizons*, no. 38, January 2004. Also Zimmerman, 'The Smoky Bomb Threat', *New York Times*, 19 December 2006.

65 This discussion has been informed, in part, by interviews with Captain Bruce Stubbs (rtd), United States Coast Guard, Washington DC, June 2004 and August 2006.

66 James Jay Carafano, 'Missing the Real Missile Threat', *The Washington Post*, 26 July 2006, available at http://www.wash-ingtonpost.com/wp-dyn/content/article/2006/07/25/AR2006072500705.html.

67 Randall J. Larsen, 'Rethinking Border Security', The Institute of Homeland Security White Paper, 1 November 2005, pp. 3–5, available at http://tihls.org/White_Paper__Rethinking_Border_Security_1_Nov_05.pdf.

68 Jon Fox, 'US Nuclear Detection Official Doubts Threat by Sea', NTI Global Security Newswire, 25 May 2007, available at http://www.nti.org/d_newswire/issues/2007_5_25.html#30A5C1DB.

69 J. Ashley Roach, 'PSI and SUA: An Update', paper presented to the 31st Virginia Law of the Sea Conference, Max Planck Institute, Heidelberg, Germany, 24–26 May 2007.

70 See Sean Boyne, 'Uncovering the Irish Republican Army', *Jane's Intelligence Review*, 1 August 1996, available at http://www.pbs.org/wgbh/pages/frontline/shows/ira/inside/weapons.html.

71 Graham Usher and Julian Borger, 'Israel Halts Palestinian Arms Ship', *Guardian*, 5 January 2002, available at http://www.guardian.co.uk/israel/Story/0,2763,628003,00.html. For more details on this and a previous incident that was not necessarily related to Iran, see Kirill and Oleg Granovsky, 'Weapons Found on the *Karine-A* and *Santorini*', WarOnline, 20 July 2002, available at http://www.waronline.org/en/analysis/pal_weapons.htm.

72 Richardson, *A Time Bomb for Global Trade: Maritime-Related Terrorism in an Age of Weapons of Mass Destruction*, pp. 14–15.

73 See 'Israeli Navy Intercepts TNT On Way To Gaza', *The Washington Post*, 9 May 2006, for an example.

74 'Indian Navy Heightens Vigil to Check Sri Lanka Tamil Tiger Clout', Lankaeverything.com, 5 June 2007, available at http://www.lankaeverything.com/vinews/srilanka/20070605023901.php.

75 For a detailed review of the LTTE's maritime capability and its influence on other groups, see Martin N. Murphy, 'Maritime Threat: Tactics and Technology of the Sea

Tigers', pp. 6–10. See also Davis, 'Tamil Tigers Seek to Rebuild Naval Force', p. 39, and two articles by Gunaratna: 'The Asymmetric Threat from Maritime Terrorism', pp. 24–9, and 'Trends in Maritime Terrorism – the Sri Lankan Case', *Lanka Outlook*, Autumn 1998, pp. 27–9.

76 Daniel Byman *et al.*, *Trends in Outside Support for Insurgency Movements* (Santa Monica, CA: RAND Publications, 2001), p. 119.

77 Sakhuja, 'The Dynamics of LTTE's Commercial Maritime Infrastructure', pp. 3–4; Byman *et al.*, *Trends in Outside Support for Insurgency Movements*, p. 119.

78 Chalk, *Liberation Tigers of Tamil Eelam's International Organisation and Operations – A Preliminary Analysis*, Canadian Security Intelligence Service, Commentary no. 77, Winter 1999, pp. 5–6.

79 'Sri Lanka's Perspective on Maritime Security in the Region and its Relevance to the World – Sri Lanka Foreign Minister Rohitha B', *Asian Tribune*, 4 June 2007, available at http://www.asiantribune.com/index.php?q=node/6006.

80 Samuel M. Katz, *Guards Without Frontiers* (London: Arms and Armour Press, 1990), p. 154.

81 Pyeatt Menefee, *Trends in Maritime Violence*, p. 33; Jenkins *et al.*, 'A Chronology of Terrorist Attacks and Other Criminal Actions Against Maritime Targets', in B.A.H. Parritt (ed.), *Violence at Sea* (Paris: ICC Publishing, 1986), p. 66; Katz, *Guards Without Frontiers*, pp. 156 and 158.

82 *Ibid.*, p. 163.

83 For example, Andrea Felstead and Mark Odell, 'Agencies Fear Extent of Al-Qaeda's Sea Network', FT.com, 21 February 2002, available at http://specials.ft.com/attackonterrorism/FT3U47PPYXC.html; Martin Bright, Paul Harris and Nick Paton Walsh, 'Hunt for 20 Terror Ships', *Observer*, 23 December 2001, available at http://observer.guardian.co.uk/international/story/0,6903,624196,00.html; and Mintz, 'Al-Qaeda Fleet Takes Terrorist Threat to Sea', *Sydney Morning Herald*, 1 January 2003, available at http://www.smh.com.au/articles/2002/12/31/1041196641696.html.

84 Dragonette, 'Lost at Sea', p. 175. For detail on front companies, and how they could be used to disguise terrorist activities, see Rupert Herbert-Burns, 'Terrorism in the Early 21st Century Maritime Domain', in Ho and Raymond, *The Best of Times, The Worst of Times: Maritime Security in the Asia-Pacific* (Singapore: World Scientific Publishing/Institute of Defence and Strategic Studies, 2005), pp. 158–63.

85 See Pyeatt Menefee, *Trends in Maritime Violence*; Gunaratna, 'The Asymmetric Threat from Maritime Terrorism', p. 26.

86 See Paul Dillon, 'Piracy Disappears in Tsunami's Wake', AlJazeera.net, 31 January 2005.

87 Raymond, 'The Malacca Straits and the Threat of Maritime Terrorism', *PINR*, 24 August 2005, available at http://www.pinr.com/report.php?ac=view_printable&report_id=352&language_id=1.

88 'Indonesia Agrees Aceh Peace Deal', BBC News, 17 July 2005, available at http://news.bbc.co.uk/1/hi/world/asia-pacific/4690293.stm.

89 'Guide to the Philippines Conflict', BBC News, 10 February 2005, available at http://news.bbc.co.uk/1/hi/world/asia-pacific/1695576.stm, is a useful backgrounder on the various Philippine terrorist and insurgent groups.

90 Bruce Vaughn *et al.* estimate 10,000 in *Terrorism in Southeast Asia* (RL31672), Congressional Research Service, 7 February 2005, available at http://www.fas.org/sgp/crs/terror/RL31672.pdf, p. 21; Abuza, in *Balik Terrorism: The Return of the Abu Sayyaf*, p. 37, estimates 12,000.

91 For a description of ASG factions, see Banlaoi, 'Maritime Terrorism in Southeast Asia: The Abu Sayyaf Threat', p. 69.

92 Quoted in R. Hariharan, 'Sri Lanka: How Strong Are the Tigers?', South Asia Analysis Group Note No. 297, 28 February 2006, available at http://www.saag.org/%5Cnotes3%5Cnote297.html.

93 For details on base areas, see Sakhuja, 'The Dynamics of LTTE's Commercial Maritime Infrastructure', pp. 1–2.

94 For a partial yet informative source, see Sri Lanka Navy, 'SL Naval History From 1984', available at http://www.navy. lk/history/1984-to.htm.

95 V. Suryanarayan, 'Sea Tigers – Threat to Indian Security'; Sakhuja, 'The Dynamics of LTTE's Commercial Maritime Infrastructure', p. 7; N. Manoharan, 'Tigers With Fins: Naval Wing of the LTTE', article no. 1757, 31 May 2005, Institute of Peace and Conflict Studies, available at http://www.ipcs.org/ whatsNewArticle11.jsp?action=showVie w&kValue=1770&status=article&mod=b.

96 See Walter Jayawardhana, 'Tamil Tiger Leader Says Osama Bin Laden-led Al-Qaeda Copied Terrorist Tactics From Liberation Tigers of Tamil Eelam', Go2lanka.com, 12 December 2002, available at http://www.go2lanka.com/ stories/021212.html; Gunaratna, 'Sea Tiger Success Threatens the Spread of Copycat Tactics', *Jane's Intelligence Review*, vol. 13, no. 3, March 2001, pp. 12–16; and 'Sri Lanka's Perspective on Maritime Security in the Region and its Relevance to the World – Sri Lanka Foreign Minister Rohitha B'.

97 Bahukutumbi Raman, 'The Omens from Katunayake', South Asia Analysis Group Paper No. 285, 26 July 2001, available at http://www.saag.org/ %5Cpapers3%5Cpaper285.html;Sakhuja, 'The Dynamics of LTTE's Commercial Maritime Infrastructure', p. 12.

98 See Roland Buerk, 'Tamil Tigers Unveil Latest Tactic', BBC News, 26 March 2007, available at http://news.bbc.co.uk/1/hi/ world/south_asia/6496381.stm; Daly, 'LTTE: Technologically Innovative Rebels', ISN Security Watch, 5 June 2007, available at http://www.isn.ethz. ch/news/sw/details.cfm?ID=17696.

99 Katz, *Guards Without Frontiers*, p. 174.

100 For details of maritime insurgent operations against Israel, see 'Fishing Boat Explodes Near Israeli Vessel', CNN. com, 22 November 2002; Jonathan Howland, 'Israel's Navy Steps Up to Security Challenge in Wake of Gaza Pull-Out', The Jewish Institute for National Security Affairs (JINSA) Online, 31 May 2006, available at http://www.jinsa. org/articles/articles.html/function/view/ categoryid/154/documentid/3417/history/ 3,2360,654,154,3417.

101 Arieh O'Sullivan, 'On Guard Off Gaza's Coast', *Jerusalem Post*, 5 July 2002; Howland, 'Israel's Navy Steps up to Security Challenge in Wake of Gaza Pull-out'.

102 Ali Nouri Zadeh, 'Iranian Officer: Hizbollah Has Commando Naval Unit', *Asharq al-Awsat*, 29 July 2006, available at http://www.asharqalawsat.com/english/ news.asp?section=1&id=5801.

103 On Hizbullah's presence in different parts of the world, see Matthew Levitt, 'Hizbollah: A Case Study of Global Reach', remarks to the conference 'Post-Modern Terrorism: Trends, Scenarios, and Future Trends', International Institute for Counter-Terrorism, Herzliya, Israel, 8 September 2003, available at http://www. washingtoninstitute.org/templateC07. php?CID=132; on one of the Argentina attacks, see 'Iran Charged Over Argentina Bomb', BBC News, 26 October 2006, available at http://news.bbc.co.uk/1/hi/world/ americas/6085768.stm.

104 Pyeatt Menefee, *Trends in Maritime Violence*, p. 97.

105 Walid Muhammad bin Attash, also known as Tawfiq bin Attash, who had once been head of bin Laden's body-guard detail, and is known to have had a role in the *Cole* bombing, claimed in his testimony to the Combatant Status Review Tribunal that it was he who had planned the attack on the USS *Cole*, bought the explosives, procured the false documents to buy the boat and recruited the bombers; http://www.defenselink. mil/news/transcript_ISN10014.pdf. See Josh White, 'Al-Qaeda Suspect Says He Planned *Cole* Attack', *The Washington Post*, 20 March 2007, available at http://www. washingtonpost.com/wp-dyn/content/

article/2007/03/19/AR2007031900653.
html and Harnden, 'Detainee "Admits
USS Cole Bombing"', *Daily Telegraph*, 20
March 2007, available at http://www.
telegraph.co.uk/news/main.jhtml?xml=/
news/2007/03/20/wgitmo20.xml.

106 Chalk, 'Maritime Terrorism in the
Contemporary Era: Threat and Potential
Future Contingencies', pp. 34–5.

107 Pelkofski, 'Before the Storm: Al-Qaeda's
Coming Maritime Campaign', p. 22.

108 Hoffman, *Responding to Terrorism Across
the Technological Spectrum* (Carlisle
Barracks, PA: US Army War College,
Strategic Studies Institute, 1994), p. 2.

109 Sinai, 'Future Trends in Worldwide
Maritime Terrorism', p. 63; Raymond,
'Maritime Terrorism, A Risk Assessment:
The Australian Example', in Ho and
Raymond, *The Best of Times, The Worst
of Times: Maritime Security in the Asia-
Pacific*, p. 208; Gunaratna, 'Al Qaeda's
Trajectory in 2003', available at http://
www.pvtr.org/pdf/GlobalAnalysis/
AQ%20Trajectory%202003.pdf.

110 Pelkofski, 'Before the Storm: Al-Qaeda's
Coming Maritime Campaign', p. 22.

111 On West's statements on the issue, see
'First Sea Lord Warns of Al-Qaeda Plot
to Target Merchant Ships', *Lloyd's List*, 6
August 2004; Sean Rayment, 'Navy Chief
Has "Too Few Ships to Guard Sea Lanes
From Terrorists"', *Sunday Telegraph*, 7

September 2003; Michael Smith, 'Navy
Steps Up Al-Qaeda Anti-Terror Patrols',
Daily Telegraph, 26 November 2002.

112 For fuller discussion of the considerations
involved, and of the reluctance on the
part of terrorists to take to the water, see
Wilkinson, 'Technology and Terrorism',
p. 172; Chalk, 'Threats to the Maritime
Environment: Piracy and Terrorism',
p. 9; Jenkins *et al.*, 'A Chronology of
Terrorist Attacks and Other Criminal
Actions Against Maritime Targets', in
Parritt (ed.), *Violence at Sea*, pp. 63–85;
Thomas S. Schiller, 'Maritime Terrorism:
The Threat', in Parritt (ed.) *Violence at
Sea*, pp. 87–92; and Pelkofski, 'Before
the Storm: Al-Qaeda's Coming Maritime
Campaign', pp. 21–2.

113 Mark J. Valencia believes that the threat of
maritime terrorism has been exaggerated
by a minority of analysts. In his view, terrorists may hope to develop major maritime capabilities, but they do not have
the experience needed to be able to do so.
Interview via email, 2004. Although the
situations are not analogous, it is perhaps
worth recalling that the fears expressed
in the early 1980s about the potential terrorist threat to offshore oil installations
have so far not been realised. See Jan S.
Breemer, 'Offshore Energy Terrorism:
Perspectives on a Problem', *Terrorism*,
vol. 6, no. 3, 1983, pp. 455–68.

Chapter Three

1 Foreign Policy and the Fund for Peace,
'The Failed States Index', *Foreign Policy*,
July–August 2005, available at http://
www.foreignpolicy.com/story/cms.
php?story_id=3098.

2 See 'The National Strategy for Maritime
Security', September 2005, pp. 16–17,
available at http://www.whitehouse.
gov/homeland/4844-nsms.pdf; David W.
Munns, '121,000 Tracks', *Sea Power*, vol.
48, no. 7, July 2006.

3 Admiral Mike Mullen, remarks to the
17th International Seapower Symposium,
Naval War College, Newport, Rhode
Island, USA, 21 September 2005, available at http://www.navy.mil/navydata/
cno/mullen/speeches/mullen050921.txt.

4 John G. Morgan and Charles W.
Martoglio, 'The 1,000-ship Navy: Global
Maritime Network', US Naval Institute
Proceedings, vol. 131, no. 11, November
2005, pp. 14–17.

5   Gurpreet S. Kuranar, '"Thousand-Ship Navy": A Reincarnation of Controversial P.S.I.?', Institute for Defence Studies and Analysis (New Delhi) *Strategic Comments*, 28 December 2006, available at http://www.idsa.in/publications/strat comments/GurpreetKhurana281206.htm.

6   For a powerful statement on these pressures and their effects on naval forces see 'Realistic' [pseudonym], 'The Route to Irrelevance – or a Wake-Up Call?', *The Naval Review*, vol. 94, no. 4, 2006, pp. 311–16.

7   For a discussion of the future maritime environment, see ONI and US Coast Guard Intelligence Coordination Center, *Threats and Challenges to Maritime Security 2020*, Chapter 3, available at http://www.fas.org/irp/threat/maritime2020/CHAPTER3.htm.

8   See Mark Huband, 'Extremists in Europe Find Fraud Pays', *Financial Times*, 15 June 2004. Interestingly, this report also quotes unnamed US officials who estimated that al-Qaeda's annual expenditure in the year of writing was closer to $10m.

9   See the US government's 'National Strategy for Combating Terrorism', pp. 7–8, available at http://www.whitehouse.gov/news/releases/2003/02/counter_terrorism/counter_terrorism_strategy.pdf; Ian O. Lesser, 'Countering the New Terrorism: Implications for Strategy', in Lesser *et al.* (eds), *Countering the New Terrorism* (Santa Monica, CA: RAND, 1999), pp. 106 and 137; Kimberley L. Thachuk, 'Terrorism's Financial Lifeline: Can It Be Severed?', *Strategic Forum*, no. 191, May 2002, pp. 1 and 3. Also J.F. Holden-Rhodes and Peter A. Lupsha, 'Horsemen of the Apocalypse: Gray Area Phenomena and the New World Disorder', *Low Intensity Conflict and Law Enforcement*, vol. 2, no. 2, Autumn 1993, p. 220: 'If you want to make a revolution … you need hard cash to do it … Bank robberies and kidnappings are still useful, but drug trafficking can generate the cash to pay the bills.'

10 'Some of the most useful intelligence [received by US investigators] on terrorists linked to al-Qaeda has been given by informers or infiltrators of criminal gangs': Huband, 'Al-Qaeda Forms Drug Links as Anti-Terror War Bites', *Financial Times*, 15 June 2004.

11 Mark A.R. Kleiman, *Illicit Drugs and the Terrorist Threat: Causal Links and Implications for Domestic Drug Control Policy*, Congressional Research Service, RL32334, April 2004, pp. 2–7.

12 For details on cooperation between the LTTE's maritime arm and criminal organisations, see Sakhuja, 'The Dynamics of LTTE's Commercial Maritime Infrastructure'.

13 On the Pentagon Gang – which the US and Philippine governments regard as a terrorist organisation, but which specialises in kidnapping-for-ransom for largely criminal purposes – see Luz Rimban, 'The Many Lives of the Pentagon Gang', *Public Eye*, vol. 9, no. 1, January–March 2003, available at http://www.pcij.org/imag/PublicEye/pentagon.html.

14 Typology based on Chris Dishman, 'Terrorism, Crime and Transformation', *Studies in Conflict and Terrorism*, vol. 24, 2001, pp. 43–58, and Thomas M. Sanderson, 'Transnational Terror and Organized Crime: Blurring the Lines', *SAIS Review*, vol. 24, no. 1, Winter–Spring 2004, pp. 49–61.

15 For more on criminal–terrorist convergence, see Barry R. McCaffrey and John A. Busso, 'Narcotics, Terrorism, and International Crime: The Convergence Phenomenon', in Russell D. Howard and Reid L. Sawyer (eds), *Terrorism and Counterterrorism: Understanding the New Security Environment* (Guildford, CT: McGraw-Hill/Dushkin, 2003), p. 210.

16 For a description of the system, see OECD Maritime Transport Committee, *Security in Maritime Transport: Risk Factors and Economic Impact*, pp. 25–9.

17 Alfred Thayer Mahan, [1890] *The Influence of Sea Power Upon History, 1660–1783* (New York: Dover, 1987), p. 25.

18 Sakhuja, 'Indian Ocean and the Safety of Sea Lines of Communication', pp. 688–9.

19 Because hub ports 'collect' numerous trades at a single concentrated point, they possess some of the attributes of chokepoints; suffering similar vulnerabilities to blockage, intended or otherwise. Additionally, the IT systems that enable these ports to achieve their huge throughput are vulnerable to sabotage by terrorists. If these systems are disrupted, the port shuts down. See Daniel Y. Coulter, 'Globalization of Maritime Commerce: The Rise of Hub Ports' in Sam J. Tangredi (ed.), *Globalization and Maritime Power* (Washington DC: National Defense University Press, 2002), pp. 133–41; also Lee Cordner, 'Maritime Terrorism: The Next "Soft Target"', *Defence and Foreign Affairs Daily*, 9 December 2003.

20 Though the oil markets became very nervous following attacks carried out in 2004 by al-Qaeda on oil installations in Saudi Arabia. The first, on the Red Sea port of Yanbu (which took place a week after the attempted suicide boat attack on the oil terminal at Basra), elicited relatively little response. However, the price of oil increased sharply after the second attack, in Khobar, as did the level of rhetoric about the likelihood that al-Qaeda was pursing a policy of 'oil terrorism'. On the Yanbu attack, see 'Al-Qaeda Strikes at US–Saudi Oil', *DEBKAfile* Special Report, 4 May 2004, available at http://www.debka.com/article.php?aid=837. On the Khobar attack and the subsequent oil price rise, see Robin Gedye, 'Al-Qaeda Rampage Ends in Bloody Gunfight', *Daily Telegraph*, 31 May 2004; and David Litterick, 'Petrol Soars to £1 a Litre Amid Fears of Oil Terrorism', *Daily Telegraph*, 2 June 2004.

21 Though on a smaller scale, the terror threat already places burdens on the industry. Yonah Alexander and Tyler Richardson in 'He Who Commands the Sea …', *Jerusalem Post*, 19 December 2002, comment that 'the added costs placed on oil companies and insurance brokers reduce the flow of oil into the global market, far outweighing the cost accrued from [any] physical damage to the vessels'.

22 On the dependence of efficiency drives on never-ending inexpensive security, see Anna Bernasek, 'The Friction Economy', *Fortune*, vol. 145, no. 4, 18 February 2002.

23 P. Damas, 'Supply Chains at War', *American Shipper*, 1 November 2001.

24 See Bernasek, 'The Friction Economy', pp. 104–10 for a discussion of Closs's study. For a discussion of JIT, see OECD Maritime Transport Committee, *Security in Maritime Transport: Risk Factors and Economic Impact*, p. 20, and Richardson, *A Time Bomb for Global Trade: Maritime-Related Terrorism in an Age of Weapons of Mass Destruction*, p. 67. In my correspondence with Closs in August 2004, discussing the figures in the Logistics Institute's annual *State of Logistics* report that showed an increase in stockholdings, but not to the extent he had predicted, Closs remarked that while '[the report's] numbers don't reflect increases to the degree that we expected, a major source of the differences [is] lower demand for fuel [reduced transportation expense] and [the report's] assumptions regarding inventory carrying cost. The actual interest rates turned out to be much lower than most of us expected.'

25 Ramadas Rao and Tony Chan, 'Malacca Nations Shocked into Anti-Pirate Action', *Fairplay*, 11 August 2005. Also several interviews with anonymous sources, August 2005–February 2006.

26 For a detailed account of this episode, see Martin N. Murphy, 'Slow Alarm: The Response of the Marine Insurance Industry to the Threat of Piracy and Maritime Terrorism', pp. 7–10; on the decision to remove the strait from the PER list see 'Money Talks', *Fairplay*, 17 August 2006. The necessity of maintaining the pressure was emphasised by the IMB. See ICC Piracy Report, 2006, p. 16.

[27] See Margaret T. Wrightson, 'Maritime Security: Enhancements Made But Implementation and Sustainability Remain Key Challenges', testimony before the US Senate Committee on Commerce, Science, and Transportation (GAO-05-448T), Washington DC, 17 May 2005, p. 6, available at http://commerce.senate.gov/pdf/gao-port.pdf.

[28] See Martin N. Murphy, 'The Blue, Green and Brown: Insurgency and Counter-Insurgency on the Water', *Contemporary Security Policy*, vol. 28, no. 1, April 2007, pp. 63–79.

[29] This section was shaped by a valuable discussion with David Kilcullen, Chief Strategist, Office of the Coordinator for Counterterrorism, US State Department, September 2006.

[30] See 'Sea Base', Navy Warfare Development Command, available at http://www.nwdc.navy.mil/Concepts/Sea_Basing/SeaBasing.aspx.

[31] 'US 7th Fleet to Provide Naval Support for Aceh Province', *Navy Newsstand*, 1 January 2005, available at http://www.news.navy.mil/search/display.asp?story_id=16477. For more details on what became known as *Operation Unified Assistance*, see Bruce A. Elleman, *Waves of Hope: The US Navy's Response to the Tsunami in Northern Indonesia*, Newport Paper no. 28 (Newport, RI: Naval War College Press, 2007).

[32] 'Navy Gears Up for Sea-borne Terrorist Attack', Rediff.com, 29 May 2007, available at http://www.rediff.com/news/2007/may/29navy.htm.

[33] 'Southeast Asia's Tri-Border Blackspot', *Jane's Terrorism and Security Monitor*, May 2007, pp. 10–11.

[34] See Andrew Exum, *Hizballah at War: A Military Assessment*, Policy Focus no. 63 (Washington DC: The Washington Institute for Near East Policy, December 2006).

[35] Mullen, remarks delivered to the 17th International Seapower Symposium.

[36] Thachuk and Tangredi, 'Transnational Threats and Maritime Responses', in Tangredi (ed.), *Globalization and Maritime Power*, p. 60.

[37] See Chalk, *Grey-Area Phenomena in Southeast Asia: Piracy, Drug Trafficking and Political Terrorism*, p. 5, where he notes that this definition is based on an idea developed first by Holden-Rhodes and Lupsha in 'Horsemen of the Apocalypse: Gray Area Phenomena and the New World Disorder', pp. 212–26. For more discussion of the new kinds of security threats facing the world, see Moisés Naím, 'Five Wars We're Losing', *Foreign Policy*, January–February 2003, pp. 28–37, and Paul J. Smith, 'Transnational Security Threats and State Survival: A Role for the Military?', *Parameters*, August 2000, pp. 77–91.

[38] For more on the relationship between criminals and terrorists, see Canadian Centre for Intelligence and Security Studies, 'Actual and Potential Links Between Terrorism and Criminality', ITAC Presents: Trends in Terrorism Series, volume 2006-5, p. 2, available at http://www.csis-scrs.gc.ca/en/itac/itacdocs/2006-5.pdf.

[39] I am indebted to Sam Bateman for crystallising this notion for me.

[40] Martha Crenshaw, 'The Causes of Terrorism', *Comparative Politics*, vol. 13, no. 4, July 1981, pp. 382–3.

[41] Quoted in Nathaniel Xavier, 'No Terrorism Threat in Straits', *The Star Online*, 5 July 2004.

[42] The original theory was put forward in 1982 by James Q. Wilson and George L. Kelling in 'Broken Windows' in *Atlantic Monthly*, available at http://www.manhattan-institute.org/pdf/_atlantic_monthly-broken_windows.pdf. See also Martin N. Murphy, Maritime Terrorism: The Threat in Context', *Jane's Intelligence Review*, vol. 18, no. 2, February 2006, p. 25.